ADOPTIN
ABUSED

Child Care Policy and Practice Series
General Editor: John Triseliotis
　　　　　　　Director of Social Work Education
　　　　　　　University of Edinburgh

Adopting or Fostering
a Sexually Abused Child

by
Catherine Macaskill

B. T. Batsford Ltd · *London*
in association with
British Agencies for Adoption and Fostering

© Catherine Macaskill 1991
First published 1991
Reprinted 1993

Typeset by Deltatype Ltd, Ellesmere Port, S. Wirral
and printed in Great Britain by
Redwood Books, Trowbridge, Wilts

Published by B T Batsford Ltd
4 Fitzhardinge Street, London W1H 0AH

A CIP catalogue record for this book is
available from the British Library

ISBN 0 7134 6760 6

Contents

Acknowledgements

This study would not have been possible without the help of several people: the Consumers' Association which funded the project; colleagues in social services departments and voluntary agencies who enabled me to set up the study; foster carers and adopters who took part in interviews and from whom I learned so much.

Special thanks to John Paley, Department of Social Policy, Cranfield Institute of Technology for formally supervising the project, and the following professional colleagues who spent many hours reading the manuscript and whose critical comments I valued highly – Phillida Sawbridge, Thea Thomson, Mary McKenna and Gerrilyn Smith. I would also like to thank Marie Leslie who painstakingly prepared the typed manuscript.

Finally, my husband Calum who often encouraged me to persevere when the children's experiences of sexual abuse evoked so much personal distress for me that it seemed as if it would not be possible to complete the task.

Note
All the material used in this book is based on real life situations. All original names have been altered for the purposes of confidentiality.

Preface

During 1989 I was awarded the Which Jubilee Award through the Consumers' Association in order to undertake this study about sexually abused children. Funding was available for a limited period of six months. This particular study proved to be far too ambitious to complete within such a short timescale. The total project in fact extended to 15 months.

All the information contained in this book was obtained through interviews with foster and adoptive families. The sample of families was not drawn together in a sophisticated scientific manner. Instead, they are a random selection of people who have one striking feature in common: they can all talk from personal experience about what it is like to live daily with children who have been sexually abused. The experiences of families are collated together as a means of providing information for other substitute families and also as a basis for guiding professional practice forward. Reading this book will at times be very painful as the trauma which some children have suffered is exposed and as the impact of sexual abuse makes an indelible impression on the reader's mind.

This is not intended to be a theoretical text book. Its aim is to be as practical as possible; many foster and adoptive families who took part in this study complained that so much literature about sexually abused children was abstract and divorced from the reality of daily living. In order to keep the text as straightforward as possible, this book confines itself to describing only the day-to-day experiences of substitute families who took part in this particular study and does not go on to compare or contrast the material with other studies about sexually abused children which are already published.

This book, therefore, is immediately relevant for all foster and adoptive families, social workers and all other professionals working in this specialist area. It also has information to share with anyone who is concerned about children whose lives have been so deeply affected by sexual abuse.

Catherine Macaskill

1 *Introduction*

Sexual abuse of children is a subject which evokes strong emotions. This study took place during 1989, in the aftermath of the Cleveland enquiry which focused so much public attention on this theme. Dilemmas and conflicts associated with this area of professional practice have been well rehearsed. Questions have been asked. Few concrete answers have been given. Much time has been concentrated on the sensitive issues surrounding the diagnosis of child sexual abuse and subsequent planning for children. Limited time has been available to focus on the needs of foster and adoptive families who may face the challenging task of parenting or re-parenting such children.

No one denies that the reported incidence of child sexual abuse has increased. Statutory and voluntary agencies with responsibility for childcare work have been caught unawares and forced to respond. More and more children carrying the overt label 'sexually abused' have been referred to Social Services Departments because their own families have been unable to provide them with adequate care and protection. No time has been available, however, to recruit new foster and adoptive families with a special aptitude for this work. The idea of providing training in child sexual abuse for experienced families has been discussed and rediscussed. With professional time, energy and resources already stretched to their maximum in the childcare field, it is not surprising to discover that in many areas the notion of training has stagnated. Despite this, it seems obvious that if families are to engage effectively in this difficult work, they are likely to require not only immense sensitivity but also a degree of specialist knowledge and skill.

The outcome of this situation has been that foster and adoptive families with no previous experience of caring for abused children have had to rise to the challenge of this important work. In the absence of training, there has been a heavy dependence on intuitive hunches rather than a reliable body of knowledge. Inherent in this work are additional stresses because the diagnosis of sexual abuse is often clouded by uncertainty and in some cases completely concealed. The reality is that any foster or adoptive family may suddenly be faced with a child whose language or behaviour provides the first clue that sexual abuse has occurred.

The 1980s have witnessed a unique period in the history of adoption/ fostering and child sexual abuse. Clearly there are lessons to be learned. It would be a mistake to allow this decade to pass without learning from families who have been so close to the task. This study is therefore an attempt to gain knowledge by listening to the experience of adoptive and foster families of sexually abused children.

A SEARCH FOR FOSTER AND ADOPTIVE FAMILIES TO INTERVIEW

Twenty-two social services departments and 12 voluntary agencies were invited to nominate adoptive and foster families with experience of parenting sexually abused children. Some departments failed to reply; some responded saying that they had 'no appropriate families for this type of study'; others delayed so long during the negotiation stage that they had to be excluded because of time constraints. Eventually, 11 social services departments and 8 voluntary agencies agreed to take part, each nominating a small nucleus of three to six families. The total sample comprised 66 families. The majority lived in London and the Home Counties. Five families lived in Scotland: in Edinburgh and the surrounding area.

Four families whose names were submitted declined to take part. Two were unexpectedly preoccupied with difficulties concerning another placement at the time the interview was scheduled to occur; one family excluded themselves because they did not perceive their child as sexually abused; while another shyly admitted that they would find it too embarrassing to discuss sexual issues with an outsider.

To be eligible to take part in this study, every family was required to have had at least one experience of parenting a sexually abused child. A wide variety of experience was represented. At one end of the spectrum were foster and adoptive families who had only cared for one sexually abused child. At the other extreme were foster carers with substantial experience, extending in some cases to as many as 12 placements. As the aim of the study was to learn from experienced carers, it seemed logical to include a wide spectrum of substitute family care. The study therefore comprised short term fostering, long term fostering and adoption.

Restrictions had to be placed on the study because finance was only available for a limited period of six months. This had several disadvantages:

a) the study focused solely on interviews with foster and adoptive parents. It was not possible to include interviews with social workers, although this would undoubtedly have added a fuller and more balanced perspective on some key issues;
b) questions concerning foster and adoptive families' views on professional services centred principally on the social worker's role. No attempt was made to undertake a comprehensive study of the roles of all the other professionals concerned with sexually abused children;
e) cultural issues were not addressed. In order to study the subject of sexual abuse from the perspective of different ethnic groups, it would have been necessary to have different cultures represented in the sample. Time did not allow for this type of detailed study to be undertaken.

DEFINING SEXUAL ABUSE

At the outset of the study, the term 'sexual abuse' was not defined. Faced with general information about the broad aims of this study, statutory and voluntary agencies decided themselves which families should be included or excluded. Consequently they were using their own criteria to define sexual abuse. As a result, the families nominated had often handled placements where sexual abuse was an unmistakeable and significant feature. Even when sexual abuse was concealed at the point when the placement occurred, it often emerged later as a very prominent factor.

The following definition of sexual abuse is very practical. It applies to this study because every feature of the quotation was portrayed somewhere in the interviews:

> Sexual abuse means the forcing of sexual contact. This can involve handling the child's genitals or requests for sexual handling by an older child or adult. Sometimes the contact is oral sex. Sexual contact includes attempts at penetration of the vagina or anus. Sometimes actual penetration occurs. It can involve penetration by penis but also fingers and objects can be used. Some assaults involve no physical contact. A child may be forced to look at the genitals of an older child or an adult, forced to watch adults having sex, forced to perform

sexual acts in front of adults, forced to undress or otherwise expose themselves.[1]

Within the context of this study, it was rare for children to be mere observers of sexual activity. The norm was for them to be intimately involved in some type of sexual act ranging from touching and fondling through to full sexual intercourse. The histories of the children made distressing reading. Anal, oral or vaginal abuse were sometimes associated with cruelty. Physical objects such as knitting needles, toothbrushes, knives and sticks were all used in children's genital areas. Torture featured in some cases. Restraining children, tying them to beds, gagging, shaving and burning pubic hair were additional distressing aspects. Some children had grown accustomed to being a regular part of the sexual act between parents. Sex rings occurred, with a complex network of grandparents, uncles, aunts, cousins and their associates participating in sexual rituals with all age groups of children. Young children's bodies were sold for financial rewards. Children as young as seven or eight years were themselves forced to attempt sexual intercourse while the act was videoed and later sold as pornographic material.

Every aspect of sexual abuse was not necessarily associated with pain and cruelty. The fact that there were enjoyable aspects did not make life easier. In some cases it merely added confusion and tension to the child's internal turmoil.

Questions were raised about whether the publicity surrounding Cleveland had merely exacerbated problems for children by instigating new ideas in some adults' minds. Cleveland illustrated the professional clamour which an allegation of sexual abuse can provoke. For one parent to concoct an allegation of sexual abuse against another is clearly an effective way of inciting frenzied action. This was well illustrated in the case where one parent of a child aged three alleged that her estranged partner was the abuser. The child had been forced by her mother to fabricate a story of sexual abuse and, in a distraught state, record her story over and over again on tape for officials. Behind this allegation lay a sinister and complex intrigue with one parent using sexual abuse as a weapon against another and hoping that criminal proceedings would be initiated.

Naturally the intensity of cases in this study varied considerably. In some, clear accounts of what had actually happened were obscured and substitute families were struggling in the dark in the absence of precise information.

[1] ADAMS, CAREN and FAY, JENNIFER, *No More Secrets. Protecting Your Child From Sexual Assault*, Impact Publishers, 1981.

QUESTIONS TO BE ADDRESSED THROUGH THIS STUDY

The study set out to obtain knowledge from adoptive and foster families by listening to their day to day experiences. Key questions on which the study pivoted included:

a) What kind of difficulties do sexually abused children cause within the context of foster and adoptive families?
b) How do families overcome these difficulties?
c) Do families feel able to help children talk about their abuse?
d) What effect does this type of placement have on all members of the family, including other children?
e) Are there special difficulties for families who have themselves been victims of sexual abuse?
f) Are there any rewards?
g) Are professional services perceived as effective or ineffective?
h) What type of training and support do families feel they require?
i) Are additional resources necessary to enable families to perform this task well?

METHOD OF STUDY

Figure 1(a) Type of Families

Married Couples	Single Parents*
55	11

Total: 66 Families
*Of the 11 single parents ten were women and one was a man.

It was never intended that this study would be dependent on a scientifically devised sample of families. Its main aim was to learn from any foster or adoptive family who could talk from personal experience about day-to-day living with a sexually abused child. By listening carefully to the experiences of families, it was felt that lessons could be learned which would be valuable for other substitute families and for professionals.

A total of 66 families took part in the study. The same interview

Figure 1(b) Length of previous fostering/adoption experience

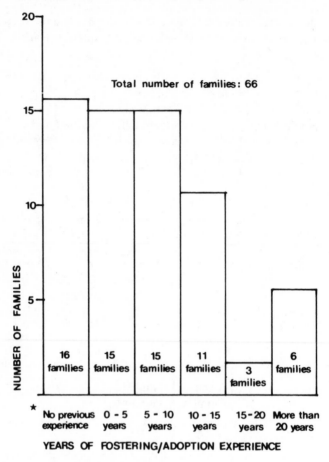

schedule was used with each family, and all were interviewed within the informal setting of their own home. Figure 1(a) indicates the type of families included. Figure 1(b) highlights how experienced or inexperienced families were in the field of substitute family care. An interesting cross-section of families was represented. Some who had considerable experience of caring for sexually abused children had thought deeply

16

about the issues in the questionnaire. Others who were relatively new to this work were eager to hear any information from the study which would assist them.

Due to constraints of time it was not always possible to interview both partners. Of the 55 couples, 26 were joint interviews. The remaining 29 were with adoptive and foster mothers on their own. This inevitably constituted some loss of the male perspective on the subject of sexual abuse. Even when joint interviews occurred, it was questionable whether the male perspective was always fully verbalized. The fact that all the interviews were conducted by myself as a female interviewer inevitably influenced the information obtained.

In order to keep the interview as clear as possible, it seemed appropriate to focus the interview on one placement only. Families with considerable experience were asked to select the placement which in their opinion had been most interesting. Some chose to talk about a placement which had disrupted, others focused on the most difficult or most rewarding one. A number preferred to discuss a current placement in the hope that talking about it might help them to disentangle the threads of difficulty running through it. Of course, families with only one experience did not have this choice. In situations where siblings had been placed, interviews focused on the sibling group. In this way a total of 80 placements were studied in some depth.

With very experienced families, it was impossible to penetrate the full depth of their experience and knowledge in one interview. The fact that the interview focused only on one placement was slightly restricting for them. Some were clearly disappointed that the interview was brought to a close after a couple of hours. They would have welcomed the opportunity to talk in similar detail about other placements which they had tackled and from which they had learned so much.

The families who took part in this study were predominantly white. Two black families were nominated but one declined to take part. Two

Figure 2(a) Age of Children at Time of Placement

Under 5 years	5–11 years	11–18 years
18	30	32

Total number of children: 80

placements concerned black children placed transracially with white foster families. This study does not claim to be representative of families in Britain today, nor does it represent the viewpoint of families from different ethnic backgrounds.

Figure 2(b) Sex of Children

Boys	Girls
30	50

Total: 80

As more information is currently available on sexually abused girls than boys, it was helpful that a considerable number of families chose to talk about the placement of a boy.

Length of placement

Placements stretched over periods from three months to seven years. One exception was a fostering placement included because of interesting features despite the fact that it had only lasted for three days. Exactly 50 per cent of children studied had been in placement for less than one year. The longest placement was seven years.

Of the placements 77 were made between 1985 and 1989. The remaining three occurred between 1982 and 1984.

ADDITIONAL FACTORS IN CHILDREN'S BACKGROUND HISTORIES

Sexual abuse was only one factor in each child's history. Consequently, it needs to be viewed within the context of a multiplicity of problems. Many children had lived in impoverished family environments with the quality of parental care only too frequently being called into question. A number of children were on 'At Risk' registers due to injuries such as bruising, burning, inexplicable fractures or in some cases just a general professional dissatisfaction with the level of physical and emotional care. Sometimes concern about another sibling was the trigger which sparked off care proceedings for the entire family. Alcoholism, drug addiction and mental illness were factors appearing and reappearing on family case records. In situations where one parent had turned to prostitution, children frequently witnessed or were part of the harassment or physical cruelty associated with this lifestyle. Murder of another child or adult occurred more than once in the study and was sometimes the crisis which led to 'reception into care'. In one case an eight-year-old boy watched his father commit suicide.

Rehabilitation with the natural family rarely succeeded. Only in five of the 80 placements had this plan been even moderately successful. In one case where there were high hopes of successful rehabilitation, it had failed abysmally because the mother had chosen to re-admit the perpetrator to the family home. It was noticeable that there was only one child successfully rehabilitated with her own family where the alleged abuser continued to live as a permanent family member.

For many children, reception in and out of care had become a way of life. Of the 80 children 58 had previous experience of either being in residential care or some type of family placement. Disruption of an adoption or fostering placement at an earlier stage had been experienced by 26 children. It was interesting to note that earlier disruptions were often related to a sexual issue. Examples varied, but included a boy propositioning an adoptive mother to kiss his penis; a child discovered cuddling another foster child's breasts; girls masturbating together in the bath; a nine-year-old boy kissing a picture of a nude woman on page three of a newspaper. It was not always the substitute family who requested that the placement terminate. In some situations, social services departments had to intervene on a sexual issue. In several cases, this had involved a single parent placement where it was alleged that a male friend had tried to force sexual contact with a child.

Figure 3 Type of Family Care

Short-term fostering	Long-term fostering	Adoption Placements
40	17 (6 placements in this group began as short-term or bridge placements)	23 (5 placements in the adoption sector began as short-term or bridge placements)

Total: 80

A small proportion of long-term fostering or adoption placements began as emergency, short-term or bridge fostering placements. In these cases, the plan for the child altered as it became apparent that birth families were not in a position to re-assume parental care. Foster families then decided to make a permanent commitment to the child.

Only seven children had been formally adopted. Five of these adoption placements had been made through voluntary agencies. Within the statutory sector there seemed to be an immense ambivalence about achieving adoption. In cases where the original plan had changed from fostering to adoption, professionals often assumed that the task of adoption would be too onerous for the family, even though the family themselves were wholeheartedly committed to it.

Disruptions

Ten of the placements studied had disrupted and an additional placement was on the brink of collapse at the time when the family were interviewed for this study.

THE ABUSER

Figure 4 illustrates that in every case, the abuser was either a member of the immediate family, extended family or already known either to the family or child. Abuse by the father was the most common form. Sometimes the father was actively abusing, but the mother was going as far as physically restraining the child to enable abuse to occur. Mothers were the sole or predominant abuser in only two cases. Both concerned boys and in each situation the mother had an associated alcohol problem. A church worker who was convicted of abuse had originally become involved with the family in a helping capacity, but eventually became implicated with adult family members in a sex ring.

There were eight cases of abuse occurring within other foster or adoptive families, with the perpetrators either being the foster or adoptive parents, an older sibling or a male friend of the family. Sometimes fostering abuse did not come to light until after an adoption placement had taken place. Professionals who had been responsible for the original placement were often aghast and liable to accuse the new family of a misguided diagnosis.

Very few cases were substantiated in court. In only 15 out of 80 cases

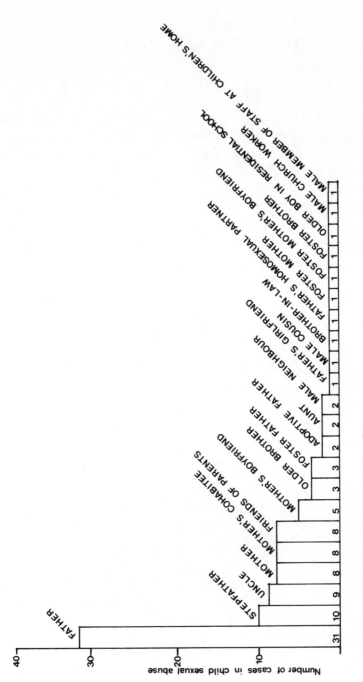

Figure 4 Who is the abuser or alleged abuser?

21

(19 per cent) was there any type of criminal conviction. In one case, however, as many as nine people were imprisoned. Cases were frequently dropped because there was insufficient evidence. Sometimes children withdrew their story or were pressurized by their own family to remain silent. When the child's disclosure occurred after being placed for adoption, the adoptive family were often reluctant to instigate criminal proceedings in case it would create a degree of distress which would impede the progress of the placement.

2 Background information in sexual abuse: what do substitute families require?

Twenty-four out of 66 families (36 per cent) were satisfied with the background information about sexual abuse which they received. Praise for social workers was effusive. This group was characterized by comments like 'I couldn't have expected more'; 'It was comprehensive. Nothing was held back'; 'They gave it to me in digestible bits. It was very constructive'. Many families who felt positively about the way in which information had been shared mentioned the value of having written reports. In some cases, this included direct access to case files. One foster mother who had substantial experience of caring for 'hard to place' children felt that within her authority, sexual abuse cases were handled more efficiently than others, with immense care being taken by professionals to share detailed information in a sensitive and thorough manner.

Figure 5 Families' verdict on the quality of information received

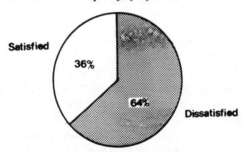

Such positive comments, however, where not reflected in all interviews. Of the 66 families 42 (64 per cent) expressed varying degrees of disappointment and frustration concerning access to background details. Some made no secret of the fact that what they perceived as professionals withholding vital background information had seriously impeded the effectiveness of their work.

SEXUAL ABUSE: A PROFESSIONAL SECRET

Sometimes the basic fact that the child had been sexually abused was concealed from the family even when professionals were clearly in possession of this information. Social workers did not always consider that it was relevant to mention sexual abuse even when it was a key factor surrounding the child's reception into care: 'The feeling they gave us was that they were not telling us for our benefit. It wouldn't be good for us to know.'

Other families conceded that the information was omitted through professional thoughtlessness rather than by deliberate design. In two cases, foster carers were shocked to discover information about sexual abuse for the first time through a casual remark made by a social worker at a major Case Conference. One adoptive father was adamant about the reasons why he thought the information had been witheld from his family: 'They're selling the child to us. They don't want to release the bad facts. Sexual abuse is not a good selling point.'

Sometimes the social worker was restricted by an issue of confidentiality. In these cases, the child had talked about abuse within a therapy situation. Confidentiality surrounded the therapy session and so professionals did not feel at liberty to tell the family.

On whatever basis the professional decision to withhold such key information was made, it often had dramatic consequences for families, as the following story illustrates:

> Social services placed an 11-year-old boy with me. No one told me anything about sexual abuse (I found out afterwards that they did know the full history of this case). The social worker said that he was a confused child who didn't know male from female ('Whatever does that mean?' I thought!). The social worker said that he needed lots of love and affection.
>
> So I gave him lots of cuddles. This child used to throw himself from one side of the room to the other. He would come up to me and touch my leg. I used to get the most awful vibes from that (but I kept thinking 'The social worker says "Give him love and affection"'). Then one day he turned and looked into my eyes and said 'I like you mum'. I responded 'I like you too'. Then the bombshell came. 'When

am I going to have sex with you?' All the other children were lying on the floor watching TV. They all turned round and stared . . . I was speechless.

SEXUAL ABUSE: A SOLITARY FACT

In other instances, families were told the scant fact that the child had been sexually abused: 'They've told us she's been sexually abused. They think that's sufficient. They haven't given us any details or any guidance.' The family who made the following comment felt seriously disadvantaged: 'They never told us WHO abused. WHEN abuse occurred. WHAT type of abuse. WHERE abuse happened.' Some families were unsure about whether they had the right to request additional information on such an intimate subject. They feared that their questions might be interpreted as 'prying'.

With hindsight, some families acknowledged that they had mishandled certain situations because they had not been adequately briefed by professionals. In one foster family where a child began to disclose for the first time, the family wrongly assumed that he had talked previously:

He started talking to us at the end of two weeks . . . At the time, because we had no real background, we didn't realize that he had not disclosed before. We didn't set in motion the wheels that were needed. We didn't even tell the social worker until two weeks later. We tried to calm the child down rather than encouraging him to get it out. In the end, the whole thing blew up with him having a chronic asthmatic attack.

Sometimes foster or adoptive families were suspicious that children were fantasizing about their past, but it was virtually impossible for them to extricate fact from fiction when they had received such sparse information.

The more scant the information was, the more likely families were to create situations within their own homes which mirrored children's previous experience of abuse, without even being aware of doing so. The most vivid example concerned a placement which disrupted when a foster carer and Angela (15) were together filling a hot water bottle in readiness for Angela retiring to bed. Suddenly Angela became very angry, and in a fit of rage threw the boiling water from the hot bottle straight into the foster carer's face. Later, the foster carer realized through reading the case file that a hot water bottle had been a significant part of this teenager's original experience of abuse. She had unwittingly sparked off a tension within the child that could probably have been avoided if she had had access to fuller information at an earlier stage.

While it is recognized that such specific details about a child's past are not always available, it does point to the importance of professionals obtaining as much data as possible about the circumstances surrounding a child's abuse and then openly sharing this information with foster and adoptive families.

SEXUALIZED BEHAVIOUR: AN IMPORTANT FACTOR IN THE CHILD'S HISTORY

It was not only details about children's history which were important. Information about any patterns of sexualized behaviour which the child had exhibited needed to be shared with families too. The following example illustrates the tensions which one family experienced due to unnecessary gaps in their knowledge:

> When she started acting seductively towards my husband, that really threw me. I didn't want to discuss it with anyone. When I did talk about it, they said that this behaviour had happened before. Why did they not tell me?

Some particularly vulnerable families would have experienced less trauma associated with their day-to-day handling of children if they had had more comprehensive data:

> After she talked to me about her abuse, she went through a phase when she complained all the time about passing urine and that her private parts hurt. I was worried about taking her to the doctor in case he would think that my husband had done the abuse. We lay awake for nights agonizing about whether we should take her to the doctor or not.
>
> When we asked her key worker, he said that kind of thing was a pattern with Sally, and that she always behaved in that way after talking about her abuse . . . I would say that the information we got was adequate in every area except the sexual abuse area.

There was not only an issue about what information should be shared, but also about how best to present it to families. Some social workers excelled at this and others failed abysmally. Sometimes families felt saturated with information and consequently unable to absorb the salient facts.

One family, who complained that all the information which they received was oversensationalized, provides a reminder of the need for a balanced approach.

> The information was overdramatized. It became sensational. They gave us the impression that the kids were monsters and that they would be running around stripping every adult in the house. If we hadn't been experienced foster parents, we would have taken fright. . . . Of the 90-odd foster children we have had, they came with the most horrendous labels. Perhaps they've been the easiest two we've had. It's the climate. Cleveland has put all the 'powers that be' on their toes.

ACCESS TO INFORMATION

Written information

Written information was perceived as useful. Adoptive families in particular felt that it was only too easy for the information to become blurred over a period of time and it was helpful to be able to refer to the written text. Sometimes written reports were used in unusual places: 'When things were at their worst with John, I used to go into the toilet and lock the door. I would read the written notes over and over again. It helped me to be more tolerant.'

Casefile material

Allowing families access to casefiles was a rather controversial subject. Only in rare cases was this facility automatically available. At the point of this study, some families were still vehemently pressing for this, but often without success. Those who did obtain permission to read files found it a very beneficial experience: 'Reading the file helped me to tie the different pieces of a very difficult background story together. I spent the whole day going through it. Perhaps for an inexperienced family it might have been too daunting.'

Families who were denied access to records felt that they were at a distinct disadvantage:

> We have asked the local authority if we could go through Adrian's case records. They have not even had the courtesy to respond. It was not important to us at the beginning, but now (one year after placement),

if we are ever going to be able to help Adrian sort things out. He's so muddled.

Adoptive families who were unable to read social services records were sometimes able to get access to legal documentation used in disputed adoption cases:

> A lot of the information we had got was from the child. Reading the documentation from the barrister was such a help. There were basic facts in the case which we had not known. For example, we did not know that the child's parents were related. When we read the material, I realized that there were a lot of threads we could have picked up on and used, if we had had the material sooner.

In at least one case, the documentation did arrive too late. After months of pressurizing their social services department, one adoptive family eventually gained access to casefile material 18 months after placement. By this time, their child's behavioural problems had reached crisis proportions and the placement had disrupted. Problems in receiving adequate background material was just one factor which the family felt had contributed to the breakdown.

One exasperated family who were weary of the conflicts associated with their attempts to obtain case records exclaimed: 'Social workers smile and say "We're colleagues. We're in this together" – but it doesn't feel like that. They don't respect you. We feel like clients.'

Other material

In two cases where pornographic videos and photographs had been a feature of children's histories, families felt that they should have been given the option of viewing this material to enable them to have a clearer understanding of what had actually occurred:

> It seemed as if they didn't want to say too much. We were not even given the option of seeing the pornographic photographs. The point is that we may have decided 'No', but we were not given the choice. A lot of the information was vetoed. We were not consulted. Social workers took the decisions for us.

Reports from other professionals

Most professionals received some degree of praise from families. There was one notable exception – therapists, such as psychotherapists, psychiatrists or psychologists, who were working with children on issues surrounding the trauma of sexual abuse. The fact that families were often denied any written or verbal information from therapists was an enormously controversial area. Families often had no knowledge at all of this aspect of a child's history and felt seriously disadvantaged. Some tried to fill this gap by making ardent pleas for information about the content of counselling sessions, or by requesting direct access to the therapist. Most requests were completely rejected with the declaration that what happened between the child and therapist was totally confidential. This left families angry and nonplussed about how they could be expected to help a child when a central part of the child's history remained a complete mystery.

WITH WHOM MAY FAMILIES SHARE INFORMATION ON ABUSE?

Foster and adoptive families were the first to recognize that information on sexual abuse was immensely sensitive material. Being entrusted with this information seemed to create a whole new set of problems with the question 'Whom may we tell?' remaining largely unresolved. Some complained that they had no clear guidance from professionals on this matter. Blunders sometimes occurred:

> Our main criticism would be that we had no information about whom we should impart knowledge to . . . We got new neighbours with two young children. I decided to put her in the picture about Vivien's background, including sexual abuse. The neighbour could not keep the lid on it. She told everyone . . . I think we were tending to be too overprotective of other people rather than protecting Vivien.

These types of blunders were the exception rather than the rule. More commonly, families tended to carry the full weight of the problem themselves. Some feared that even confiding in a trusted relative or friend might constitute a serious breach of confidentiality. In cases where professional support was poor, the fact that problems were so often contained within families' own four walls took its toll:

> The most awful thing was that there was no one to talk to about it. I was spending hours with her. At night I would go over and over it again in my head . . . It was tempting to tell people. By not telling, I felt that I was protecting the child. I did not want to tell anything that people might latch onto.

In some authorities, the aura surrounding confidentiality was so great that families felt very nervous about being caught in breach of this unwritten rule. Some foster carers felt that they could not themselves survive without confiding in someone outside the family, but seemed almost ashamed to admit that they had been forced to act in this way:

> I asked a couple of friends if they would support me – but you feel you are breaking confidence. It is not the way that the Authorities want it done. It feels a bit under the carpet. Confidentiality is a big issue with this Department which has never been sorted out.

Another question which remained unresolved was whether the school should be notified about children's history of abuse. Divergent views were expressed. A particularly strong opinion held mainly by adoptive families was that school staff should not be informed. Sometimes social workers opposed families on this issue. Even in adoption cases there were instances where social workers took the initiative and informed the school even though this was completely contrary to the adoptive family's wishes. In one case where a teacher suspected sexual abuse, she decided to ask the adoptive mother point blank about this, only to receive the evasive answer: 'Children with her kind of background have all sorts of problems.'

This chapter highlights the vital importance of substitute families receiving comprehensive and detailed information about each child placed in their care. This is a fundamental principle associated with good practice. It is also important to consider that there are times when background information may become a burden to the family unless they are given the opportunity to grapple with the question 'Whom may we tell?' Confidentiality must always be a significant factor underpinning placements of sexually abused children, but rigid definitions of the term may merely place the child and the family under additional pressure. An important piece of groundwork in every placement is therefore to define 'confidentiality' realistically.

KEY ISSUES RELATED TO BACKGROUND INFORMATION

Professionals	Foster and Adoptive Families
The need to share as full a case history as possible.[2]	Simple questions to ask:[2] WHO abused? WHAT type of abuse occurred?

Details on difficult behaviour should not omit any sexualized behaviour previously exhibited by the child.

Was violence used?
WHEN did abuse occur (including time of day)?
Child's age when it started?
Child's age when it stopped?
HOW did abuse occur?
WHERE did abuse occur?
What was the child's reactions to disclosure?
What words are used by the child or perpetrator to describe abuse?

Reconsider the implications of foster/adoptive families being denied access to information on a child's previous therapy.

Written material/case records – need to consider the value of families obtaining access to written records.

With whom may this information be shared?

Confidentiality – needs to be redefined in a clear and balanced manner.

What does confidentiality mean in relation to this particular placement?

---

[2] McFADDEN, EMILY, *Fostering the Child who has been Sexually Abused*, Institute for the Study of Children and Families, Eastern Michigan University, 1986.
(See Child's information Sheet Appendix C for example of important aspects substitute parents need to know about a child who has been sexually abused.)

3 Substitute families' initial reactions and adjustments

Families who had to make the greatest adjustments when they discovered that they were fostering or adopting a sexually abused child were naturally those who had had no warning prior to the placement about sexual abuse being a factor in the child's background. Figure 6 illustrates that as many as 27 placements were in this category. In six out of the 27 cases, professionals had initially withheld this vital piece of background information. In the other 21 cases, sexual abuse was a completely unknown aspect of the case which had not been previously recorded by any professional.

Figure 6 Families' knowledge about sexual abuse before or after placement

BEFORE	BEFORE	AFTER
Definite	Suspicion	
40 (50%)	13 (16%)	27 (34%)

Total: 80

Waves of panic swept through some families as it dawned on them that they were now parenting a child who had been the victim of sexual abuse. Some families were so frightened of the diagnosis that they seriously considered terminating the placement. Others reacted with disbelief: 'When it came out we were just amazed. I went around for days asking myself the question "Does this *really* go on?". Nothing like this had ever come out in our family.' Shock and bewilderment took over in some cases, leaving the family in disarray: 'We were so shocked. It must be something similar to what a woman feels when she has been raped. You don't know where to turn. Your mind goes wrong and you just can't think straight.'

During the assessment period, some foster and adoptive families had singled out the sexually abused child as the one child whom they felt unable to parent. Now they felt cheated and thrown into a situation for which they were ill-equipped:

It was a bit like saying to the hospital 'Whatever happens, do not take my leg off'. You waken up suddenly and you think . . . 'Gosh! Help! My leg has been amputated' . . . It was exactly the opposite of what we had asked for.

Foster carers who had suffered sexual abuse themselves but had kept this a closely guarded secret described their internal conflicts. Faced unexpectedly with the task of parenting a sexually abused child, some experienced an intolerable feeling of vulnerability. Hard lessons were learned through this type of placement, as one experienced foster mother revealed: 'Caring for an abused child leaves you raw. If you have covered up the fact that you have been sexually abused as a child it scrapes at the scar tissue.'

It was not only families who were faced with the unexpected news of sexual abuse who had struggles. Even families who had received a detailed sexual history were sometimes completely at sea. Receiving the facts was one thing. Knowing how to interpret them was quite another. Inexperienced families complained about being left to manage as best they could on their own without even the simplest guidelines: 'How do you handle this kind of thing? We were in the dark. No one thought to give us the Dos and Don'ts.'

CHANGES IN FAMILY LIFESTYLE

What type of changes did a sexually abused child bring about in family life? Clearly, there were a significant number for both adults and children. Families who had considerable experience of parenting other 'hard to place' children found that there were extra adjustments and stresses inherent in this type of parenting because of the sexual component. A new type of caution had to be exercised within the intimacy of family life. Touch took on a new significance and could so easily be misconstrued by the child as a sexual advance. New boundaries had to be constructed around relationships. New questions had to be addressed. Sexually abused children continued to need love and affection, but adults and children needed self-protection. One foster carer described what they were doing as 'parenting with rubber gloves on'. One question which predominated was: 'How could such deprived children be parented "at a distance" when they were so hungry for the warmth and security of physical contact?'

In families where both partners had devised a system of being equally involved in the parenting task, it was often necessary to change that balance:

> We had worked out a routine with the foster children. My husband would undress all the children. I would bath them. He would dry them. That had to change completely. He was out of it altogether. It had to be done totally by myself or my 13-year-old daughter. That was hard.

Foster mothers frequently complained that a disproportionate amount of physical care suddenly landed fairly and squarely on their shoulders:

> With this type of fostering, the fellow says 'You deal with it', so it puts it all on to the foster mum. The husband can't be on his own with the child as there's always a chance of an allegation. You just can't share the care. If it's an ordinary girl in the bath and I'm busy, I can say to my husband 'Pop your head round the door. See if she's taken the plug out of the bath'. With this type of child, he just can't do that. You have to watch all the time – and keep on top of things all the time. Emotionally and physically it wears you down.

It was not only the physical aspect of caring which placed extra stress on the foster mother. Some felt that they had to be 'eyes and ears' for their partner:

> There's a burden on the foster mother to protect the foster father. My husband's naive. He's laid back. If someone wanted to seduce him, other people would spot it immediately. He would be seduced before he knew. The woman has to perceive when the sexualized child is 'on the move'.

Another adjustment concerned childsitting arrangements. Adoptive and foster fathers could often no longer undertake this task, and certainly not single-handed:

> My husband was very careful. I never left the girls with him. One of them would follow him into the bathroom and bedroom. If my

husband was around, she just could not wait to pull her pants off and expose her bottom. He felt it was a terrible threat.

Household routines had to change. A new level of sensitivity seemed to permeate even the simplest interaction. One foster mother commented: 'Going to the toilet suddenly became an event.' Locks on bathroom doors became commonplace. Adults and children began to wear bathrobes. It was no longer permissible for anyone to appear in underwear or scantily clad. One adoptive father reflected: 'I would say that modesty became the norm.'

Children's play had to be closely monitored: 'I was very careful to leave doors open. I kept an eye on all the games played. I always made them play in the living room rather then upstairs in the bedroom.' Even night time was not a time when some families felt that they could totally switch off and forget the problem: 'You tend to be on tenterhooks all the time. At night time you're wondering "Are they doing what they should not be doing?"'

Parents had to discuss sexual issues with their children. If they had not done so previously, it now became a matter which required urgent attention. Those who delayed did so at their peril. Children were liable to be made aware of the most comprehensive sexual information, based on the real life story of the new child who had just joined the family. Several families took advantage of this time to gather all their children around them and to begin to teach them basic facts about touching and human relationships.

Perhaps the greatest conflicts concerned how to handle close physical contact with the child. The child's desperate need for physical affection, combined with the child's tendency to sexualize any form of contact, placed enormous strains on family relationships. What does an adoptive father do in the following situation? 'She was all over the top of me. She would sit on my knee and try and touch me up. She had no idea of boundaries and no respect for anyone.' What does an adoptive mother do when a teenage boy yearns for physical love, and yet all her instincts tell her that his touch is sexual?

These problems were even more pronounced when there were other children in the family, who were naturally competing for parental attention and affection. How much should life change for them? 'When our ten-year-old girl, who is hydrocephalic, was ill, she always used to creep under the covers with my husband. Should we still allow her to do that? What if the boys started doing it too?' Parents often struggled to know whether they should have one rule for the abused child and another for other children in the family, or whether they should forget the past and standardize rules for everyone.

KEY ISSUES RELATED TO PRACTICE IMPLICATIONS

During preparation, every foster and adoptive family should have the opportunity to reflect on the following:

a) the fact that sexual abuse could be a factor in the background of any child being placed for fostering or adoption;

b) ways in which a sexually abused child might interpret day to day events, familiar conversations, normal physical relationships and intimate relationships which are a regular part of their everyday living;

c) any changes which they might be required to make in their lifestyle in order to integrate a sexually abused child and the impact of these changes on everyone concerned;

d) practical arrangements for bed-time routines, bathing, toileting, supervising children's play and activities, childsitting and escorting children.

4   *Picking up the signs of sexual abuse*

It was rare for children to begin immediately to share intimate secrets of their abuse with foster and adoptive families. More frequently, the first indicators of abuse became evident through a variety of unusual behavioural signs. Recognition of these signs was vital. It was often by responding to them and using them as a basis for a conversation with the child that families became adept at helping children verbalize the story of their abuse.

Children rarely exhibited one behavioural sign in isolation. Usually several different aspects of behaviour merged together. Families who had not been aware that sexual abuse was a factor in their child's background often struggled to comprehend what was happening. Slowly an unwelcome question dawned on their mind: Is it possible that this child may have been sexually abused?

Even very young children would make sexual overtures to an adult member of the family, and yet at the same time demonstrate intense fear of any type of sexual contact. This paradoxical behaviour was very difficult for some families to fathom:

> It started that four-year-old Anne didn't like my husband to bath her. She didn't want him to see her knickers. At first, I just put it down to the fact that she was not used to him. She would come into bed with us in the mornings. She was off me, but she started being very suggestive to my husband. She seemed to be trying to provoke sexual contact, but at the same time she was very frightened. My husband was worried about it. We had had no contact with this type of thing before. We thought that she could not have got this from a child's mind.

Of course, these sexual advances were not always made to men. Foster and adoptive mothers were approached also: 'He used to start kissing my toes and then work his way up. There's stroking and *stroking*, but his was so sexual. It was very different to anything I had experienced before. It made me feel terrible.'

In other cases, sexual behaviour was directed towards other children, displaying itself either in real-life situations or in play:

He used to make inappropriate advances to the girls. He would lie on top of them and move up and down as if engaged in the sexual act. He would play hospitals. He would line up the dolls and teddy bears on the living room floor and lie on top of them as if he was having sex with them.

Other instances included a girl of 11 offering a boy of eight money for sex, or children being caught in bed together trying to engage in sexual activity. Another common factor was for children to be extremely preoccupied with their own bodily functions:

They would run about with nothing on. They were exposing themselves all the time. In the bath, they would try to pull each others' willies. They were obsessed with their privates. One of the boys kept asking us to look at it to see if it was alright . . . We had a feeling that something was wrong. We had never seen children show their bums before the way they did. The things they did were different.

Excessive masturbation was a problem in some situations. Siblings masturbated together without the slightest interest in who was observing them. Some boys masturbated to the point of causing bleeding and needed medical treatment. Girls used corners of tables or chairs to masturbate openly. One 11-year-old girl who used to masturbate over her brother's photograph made no secret of the fact that she yearned to see him again so that she could renew sexual contact with him. Another difficulty was boys masturbating privately and then hiding the evidence among other children's underclothes.

Any sense of privacy or an awareness of the need for boundaries in relationships were sometimes lacking. Some children would talk and act sexually in the most inappropriate places:

Mark is 14 years, but he has the mind of a five-year-old. To him, sex was an everyday thing. He would use any excuse to undo his trousers and pull out his penis. He would come into the bathroom when my husband was in the bath and want to sit down and chat. He had no concerns about sex being public. So much of his life, his parents had had sex in front of him. He would want to come into bed with me, and he would cry like a baby when I said 'No'.

Some children used a repertoire of sexualized language which poured out in torrents without a glimmer of concern about who might be listening. One 12-year-old boy always prefixed his sentences with obscene words, or composed instant rhymes with what his adoptive mother described as 'filthy words'. Another girl could be heard chattering to herself at bedtime with an unending stream of sexual words.

Some children became frightened or reacted hysterically in certain rooms of the house, most commonly the bathroom, toilet or bedroom which, of course, were places associated with their abuse. One boy was so terrified of closed doors that his foster-mother temporarily removed the bedroom and bathroom door in an attempt to pacify him. Other phobias concerned dress, for instance wearing clothes to bed or screaming or reacting warily at the prospect of undressing in the bedroom, but being perfectly content to undress anywhere else in the house, and shrinking from any type of physical contact. Even very young children who had experienced sexual interference would become completely rigid when attempts were made to put on a nappy.

Washing and bathing were especially troublesome for some children, who found it enormously difficult to touch their genitals or to let anyone else touch them. Some young children provided the first opening to talk about their abuse by accusing a foster or adoptive parent of being naughty when drying them after a bath. Some teenagers showed a marked hostility towards their developing body. Twelve-year-old Jennifer was found one day pressing rather vehemently on her chest with both hands. Tearfully she asked: 'If I push these boobs, will they go away?'

Night times were disturbed with children unable to sleep and often waking up for reassurance. Nightmares were common, with dreams frequently having clear sexual connotations: 'He would waken up in the middle of the night, crying and saying "A green man bit my bum". He was convinced that there was a mark, although we could never see anything.'

Eating problems also occurred with specific foods presenting a particular problem for children who had been involved in oral sex. 'Wendy hated sausages. She hated the shape of a sausage touching her mouth.' Vanilla blancmange, instant whip, salad cream, spaghetti bolognese, tomato sauce and the uncooked white of an egg had to be banned because they triggered off such distress for children who had experienced oral sex and who immediately associated the colour and texture of these foods with semen. One foster carer could not understand why her four-year-old child became so upset when she washed his hands in the downstairs toilet, but when she washed them upstairs he was perfectly happy. Several months into the placement she realized that the liquid soap downstairs reminded the child of semen; upstairs a bar of soap had been used. Another child had a similar aversion to any type of paste. When his foster mother realized that his next Sunday School lesson was going to include cutting out and pasting, she felt compelled to talk to his Sunday School teacher about his background history.

Sometimes children alluded to their experience of abuse in figurative language. This was not always immediately understood:

> John was three-and-a-half years. He used to cry and say that the snake was coming to get him. Then he would say 'The snake spits. It spits on my legs, it spits on my feet, it spits on my hands'. Then he would point to his bottom and say 'It spits on my bottom too . . .' I decided to show him a picture of a snake and a picture of a man's body. 'Which is the snake?' I asked. He didn't hesitate. He pointed straight to the man.

One experienced foster mother who had tackled some very difficult work with sexually abused children summed up the message conveyed through this chapter in the following way: 'It is mainly the behaviour that will reveal a lot. These things do not come out in the normal course of affairs in a household. LISTEN CAREFULLY TO THE BE- HAVIOUR. It may be the only language that a child can use.'

SOME BEHAVIOURAL SIGNS WHICH MAY INDICATE THAT A CHILD HAS SUFFERED SEXUAL ABUSE[3]

None of these indicators 'prove' sexual abuse. However, when a child displays any of these signs, then it is important to raise the question 'Has this child been sexually abused?'

a) Premature sexual knowledge.
b) Sexual overtures to adults, combined with a fear of sexual contact.
c) Sexual advances to other children.
d) Child's play includes a simulation of sexual acts.
e) Extreme preoccupation with genitals and genital functions.

---

[3] For readers wishing to consult up-to-date research on the subject of sexually abused children: FINKELHOR, D. and ASSOCIATES *A Source Book on Child Sexual Abuse*, Sage, 1986. FINKELHOR, D. *Child Sexual Abuse – New Theory and Research*, New York, Free Press, 1985.

f) Flaunting of genitals.

g) Excessive masturbation (alone or with sibling).

h) Lack of awareness of boundaries in sexual activity.

i) Over-familiarity with sexual words – child uses torrents of sexualized words.

j) Fear of being in bathroom, toilet, bedroom.

k) Child insisting on wearing clothes to bed.

l) Child refusing to touch own genitals or to let others touch them.

m) Nightmares. Dreams may have sexual overtones.

n) Children who have experienced oral sex may demonstrate a distaste for foods with texture or colour similar to semen, or with a shape similar to a penis.

5 Helping children talk about their abuse

DISCLOSURES PRIOR TO PLACEMENT

Sixteen out of 80 children (20 per cent) made some type of disclosure prior to placement. It was common for children initially to divulge their secret to their teacher, but in certain cases the first comments were made to the mother, a school friend, an adult friend of the family, or in one particular case to a family who were providing respite care. Some children had previously been in and out of local authority care; their confidants were more commonly a previous foster family, a member of residential staff or a field social worker. In two cases, teenagers took overdoses of barbiturates at school. When the circumstances surrounding these suicide attempts were investigated, distraught teenagers shyly admitted that they had been victims of sexual abuse within their own families over a prolonged period.

Clearly some children who struggled to verbalize the story of their abuse had no way of knowing how traumatic the consequences of their disclosure would be. Fourteen-year-old Jackie's case is a good example. Within 24 hours of first breaking down in tears with her intimate story, Jackie's world was turned upside down as she found herself being driven to an emergency fostering placement. Reception into care was the last thing that Jackie wanted to happen. Tearfully she explained: 'I wanted one thing – someone to stop the abuse. I was frightened to death of getting pregnant. What else could I do? After all, I could hardly go to the local doctor and ask to be put on the pill.'

The cost of disclosure was enormously high for this girl. She not only lost a relationship with her abuser to whom she was deeply attached, but also experienced hostility and abuse from the entire extended family who closed ranks against her, accusing her of lying and of creating irreversible damage within her family.

DISCLOSURES AFTER PLACEMENT

In 54 out of 80 placements (67 per cent), children were able at some stage to talk with their adoptive or foster families about abuse. Among this group were some children who, despite years of therapy, had never been able to tell their story previously. There did not seem to be any pattern connected with the timing of children talking. It could be weeks, months or in some cases even as long as two years after placement.

Before considering how adoptive and foster families handled disclosure, a basic question needs to be addressed. How important did families consider it to be for children to talk with them about their abuse? It was by no means the case that everyone spoke with a clear and affirmative voice on this question. Some families felt that it was central to children's healthy development that they should be able to verbalize their story of abuse. With this burning conviction, long and exhausting hours were spent with children, encouraging them to expose painful aspects of their past history. Some of the strongest advocates of this way of working were parents who had themselves suffered abuse in silence. Others were somewhat ambivalent, feeling that they should certainly not intervene in such a private matter: 'Who knows when the time is right? If children want to talk, they will do so – but in their own time and way. Children are not sausages out of a machine. Some may not be ready to talk until they reach adulthood.'

Some people's uncertain approach was clearly influenced by the way that they had handled painful experiences in their own lives: 'I feel in two minds about it. My childhood was not happy. Even still if I think about it, it upsets me. Perhaps it is better to push these things in rather than pull them out.'

A considerable number of families hesitated about embarking on this sensitive area because of a lack of confidence. Fears of mishandling the situation, of exacerbating the problem or even creating new difficulties for children as they grew into mature adults were sometimes concerns which strangled the families' potential usefulness. Some families were petrified that the child might suddenly begin to reveal lurid details of their abuse. It is not surprising that children living in such a climate frequently remained totally mute on this unmentionable subject. It was noticeable that some families who had handled sexual issues in a very creative and effective manner were sometimes the least self-assured: 'I worried every step of the way. I kept asking myself "Have I done enough?". Every time something happened, I took a deep breath, crossed by fingers, prayed and then ploughed in. Should she have had therapy? I am really not sure.'

THE TRIGGER WHICH LED CHILDREN TO TALK

A number of children began to talk about their abuse quite spontaneously at a private time like bathtime or bedtime. This was
particularly true of very young children. Perhaps being in the bathroom
or bedroom made children more aware of their own bodies and
consequently triggered memories of abuse. Intentionally or unintention-
ally, children let comments slip like 'Grand-dad used to play with my
willy'; 'It's naughty to wash my ding dong'; 'Paul used to tickle my
daisy'. Other children's songs were revealing:

> Brian's got a girlfriend.
> Daddy's got a girlfriend.
> We saw them shagging.

These comments provided excellent opportunities for parents to ask
simple questions and to help children to open up further.

Some children tested the ground by first asking a question: 'What
would happen if someone did something a long time ago – and it was a
bad thing?' After reassurance, this boy went on to say: 'My dad got
money from an old man – his ding dong was all gooey.'

A particular event could sometimes prompt a child to talk. Examples
included a chance meeting with the abuser while shopping; fear of going
to court in connection with care proceedings; apprehension about
attending a psychotherapy session; returning to a familiar house or
street; or driving past a hospital where a child had undergone a medical
examination.

Occasionally there was an element of chance involved. The setting was
unexpectedly right. One family who decided to clean all their brass
ornaments found themselves with their living-room floor strewn with
newspapers and ornaments and a child pouring out her story of abuse for
the first time. Unknown to the family, she had seen her own mother clean
brass, and the smell of Brasso had re-opened painful experiences from
her past. While watching a television programme, a child might
suddenly see a familiar object which sparked off memories about life at
home. Quite spontaneously the child's comment 'We used to have one of
these', referring to a familiar object, would be followed by details about
life at home and in particular about sexual activity which occurred in the
family.

One girl did not talk about her abuse until she had been living with her
family for 18 months. As the facts of life were being explained to her, she
made it clear that she had no interest in the female body. This contrasted

with her intense interest in the male anatomy. It quickly became apparent that she had a vivid understanding of how the male sex organs worked.

Children who had been both physically and sexually abused rarely talked about sexual abuse first. They seemed to find it easier to share details of physical cruelty and so this was usually exposed first. A lapse of time then intervened before children summoned enough courage to complete the story with sexual details.

Talking about abuse was not always so spontaneous. In at least 18 cases there was ample evidence that children would never have disclosed without direct and determined intervention from the families themselves. Maintaining that determination was not always easy for families when a disclosure was not forthcoming and children seemed to be clinging tenaciously to their secret.

Five-year-old Peter had made some kind of allegation and then quickly retracted it. His entire foster family, including all the other children, set out to help him by spending an entire weekend playing a game called 'Secrets': 'After two days it eventually came out. He said that grandad's friend had touched him up. He told us that he was frightened to tell in case his uncles would beat him up.'

In some cases there was no easy prompt. The pain was too deep rooted to respond readily to any stimuli. Sometimes it took months or even years of intensive work to unearth the trauma of the past:

> It came out over a period of a year. I used to do one hour sessions with her twice a week using the BAAF book *In Touch with Children*. It first came out when we were doing the part about the things that made you feel good and the things that made you feel dirty. I am certain that it would not have come out in the normal day to day. Things were triggered for her by these sessions. She had 'yukky' feelings about her step-father. She remembered how he used to take her to the loo and how it made her feel 'creepy'.

Occasionally disclosure came at a stage when parents felt that they had reached the end of the road. An honest declaration to the child that they could do nothing more, or confronting the child with the fact that they were failing to communicate sometimes led the child to talk about abuse for the first time.

Explosive episodes, prolonged temper tantrums and excessive sexual demands by the child preceded disclosure in some of the most difficult placements. The families' ability to hold on through such turmoil was very impressive. Ten-year-old Mark's adoption placement had all these hallmarks:

Every night I was on my own with Mark, he would have these violent tantrums. He used to attack me with a knife and threaten to stab me. I used to have to hold him and sit on him for one to one-and-a-half hours (sometimes three hours). After two to three months of this, I decided on action.

He went to bed at 10 p.m. I began asking him why he was behaving like that. He wouldn't tell. I insisted. One hour later he started telling me about the physical abuse he had suffered – how he had been locked in cupboards, hit, deprived of food and threatened with a knife. He kept saying 'You know nothing about me'. I wondered if I should mention sexual abuse. I decided 'No'.

A month later we had another abusive episode. He went to bed with Garfield. Mark loved Garfield. He couldn't go to bed without him. 'Would you sleep with Garfield tonight?' he asked. 'Would you come into bed with me?' He said that he wanted to tell me something, but I would hate him for telling me. Then he said that he just couldn't tell. I kept reassuring him.

He was leaping about all over the bed – very agitated. He was forcing himself on me sexually. He started touching me. My blood ran cold. I felt like I was being abused.

Then he started talking. He said that it had been horrible and painful – that his mum had forced him – that she had touched him, lain on top of him and tried to have sex with him. She had wanted him to touch her. She had masturbated him. Pulling his balls about had been sore.

Once some children started talking, they just could not stop, and the entire tale tumbled out. However, this was not the norm. In Mark's case, he had more to tell about other abusive incidents, about good times with his mother and about his father's part in the abuse. Like Mark, it was common for most children to divulge their story stage by stage. Some families who had been party to very intimate disclosures sensed that the child was still withholding some aspects of abuse. It took immense sensitivity to help children and teenagers delve into some of these dark recesses and find words to express adequately the turbulent feelings associated with their past.

WHEN LANGUAGE FAILS

Communication with adults was often anything but spontaneous for such abused children. Eye-to-eye contact could be awkward. Even children's physical demeanour demonstrated just how guilty and confused the whole experience of abuse had left them. Carolyn's case illustrates this:

When she would talk to me she would be very distraught. She would curl up in the foetal position in the corner of the settee. She would put her head down and her hair would be all over her face. You couldn't see her face. She would be shaking.

In cases like Carolyn's, it was not always helpful for adults to depend on verbal communication. Some children were clearly more comfortable talking indirectly through objects such as toys or dolls: 'Four-year-old Anne told her dolls all her secrets. She used to say that the dolly kept all her secrets in her nappy.'

Even teenagers sometimes took refuge in a similar type of childlike behaviour: 'It was difficult to try and get a conversation going with 13-year-old Elizabeth. She used to talk through her dolls. If she had a problem, she would leave her bedroom door open and answer you through her dolls. She would talk in a baby voice.'

Keeping animals was an excellent form of therapy. Some children preferred to talk to the cat or dog rather than confide in an adult, whom it was hard to trust.

Children's drawings could be very expressive. When five-year-old Philip was asked to draw his family, he vividly described each drawing. This prevented any ambiguity of interpretation: 'He drew his mum with no mouth (she says nothing); his step-father with no arms (he doesn't hurt me); his gran and uncle were normal. Then he drew a friend of grand-dad's with three legs, and his middle leg was enlarged.' When asked to draw a man, some children immediately drew a penis. This was yet another indicator of how sexualized their entire lifestyle had been.

Reading material for abused children was difficult to find. A number of families who came across a book entitled *A Very Touching Book*[4] prized it highly. This is how one adoptive family used it with their eight-year-old girl:

We knew that she liked books. We got *A Very Touching Book*. We left it around. She picked it up and started looking at it. She spent one-and-a-half hours with it. It was going through that book that brought the whole thing out into the open. That was the turning point . . . The pictures in the book are ambiguous – probably they were

[4] HINDMAN, JAN, *A Very Touching Book*, McClure Hindman Associates, Oregon, 1984.

designed that way on purpose. She saw sexual relationships in the pictures that you and I would never see.

Writing letters suited some teenagers better than talking. Often they were left in places where foster or adoptive parents were bound to find them: 'She would leave letters in drawers in the house where she knew that I would find them with comments like "What if I hear people doing it?"' Others found it easier to give vent to their innermost feelings by using a typewriter, rather than talking directly to an adult or using their own handwriting. The degree of anonymity associated with typewritten words or phrases made it easier to reveal painful memories.

THE EFFECT OF DISCLOSURE ON CHILDREN

The effect on children of being able to talk about their abuse was always positive. Often there were dramatic changes in children's demeanour and behaviour, which had a beneficial outcome for the entire family. One family commented: 'You could see the relief on his face. It was as if a big weight had fallen off his shoulders.' Another foster carer's ten-year-old natural daughter came into the room while her mother was taking part in this research interview. She was eager to add her perspective: 'Mum, do you remember? It was just like you had lifted a brick off his head.'

What were the changes which occurred? Disturbed sleep patterns and nightmares became less common. In fact some children slept peacefully for hours immediately after disclosure. Excessive masturbation gradually faded or ceased completely. In one case, the problems of enuresis which had persisted throughout the entire placement stopped completely for several weeks. Temper tantrums subsided. Sexualized behaviour became much less prominent. Children became more relaxed and began to behave in a more appropriate childlike manner. In some cases, it was amazing to discover just how many positive changes occurred simultaneously:

We noticed changes almost immediately. Within days, he was no longer frightened of going to the toilet. He showed no fear when my husband bathed him. Previously he had been so wary. He started joining in games. Before, any type of rough and tumble game with physical contact terrified him. He started laughing in an ordinary way. He had not been able to cry before. After he told us he was able to cry for the first time.

Some families enthused about what had happened. They felt that they had taken the first crucial step in breaking through the emotional barricade which children had constructed around themselves: 'After she talked, she began to make attachments to us. Before that, there seemed to be a glazed look in her eyes. Afterwards, you could see a sparkle in her eyes – as if you could see a bit of life for the first time.'

THE EFFECT OF DISCLOSURE ON ADULTS

The families who suffered the greatest degree of dismay and bewilderment when disclosure occurred were undoubtedly those who had not known about the sexual abuse diagnosis prior to the placement. Other families found it distressing too. Comments like 'It was emotionally shattering'; 'I felt uncomfortable'; and 'It made me feel agitated' were typical. When children found it painful to talk, foster and adoptive families usually found it stressful too. Some reported that the most wounding aspect for them was listening to such a sordid tale in the simple language of a child. Training helped. Those families who had spent time on the topic 'Handling Disclosure' as part of a wider training programme on child sexual abuse were able to apply the knowledge and insights which they had acquired. Some families attributed their ability to remain calm and to feel confident about the appropriateness of their responses to the child as an immediate consequence of training.

A small number of children posed particular problems. They made no secret of the fact that the experience of sexual abuse had been predominantly pleasurable for them. Some families were still wondering how they should respond to such children's questions: 'Twelve-year-old Richard asks me "How do I live without sex? – How do I survive without the feelings?" He enjoyed some parts of his abuse. I find it hard to answer.'

In another case, Diane, a teenager with very limited intellectual ability, made no secret of the fact that she yearned to renew a sexual relationship with her step-father. Diane appeared to be totally uninterested as her foster family tried to explain about appropriate and inappropriate sexual relationships to her:

Books didn't help us. All the books that are written are about children being devastated by sexual abuse. Diane enjoyed it. It was OK in her eyes. She will not accept that it's wrong. When we did the life story book, I tried to explain everything, but Diane has fixed ideas and you cannot change them. Repeating it over and over again seems to make no difference. After a three year placement with us, you can go over it and she will still not remember.

Diane's foster family felt that her inability to grasp basic concepts was partially due to her limited intelligence. Intertwined with that was her complex sexual history. Later, there were serious consequences associated with her lack of understanding. One evening she disappeared; following a police alert, she was found in a neighbour's flat. There was evidence that a sexual relationship had occurred.

Mothers often carried the greatest strain. Children frequently confided in them first. In adoption placements in particular, valiant efforts were sometimes made by mothers to help the child communicate with fathers too. Often these painstaking efforts had positive results even if children sometimes decided to tell their story at the most inopportune moment:

> She would only tell me. She used to say 'I'll tell daddy when he comes home', but she never could. Then after she had been with us for about nine months, we were driving along on a busy motorway when a little voice came from the back seat of the car 'I want to tell my story to daddy'. We came off the motorway, stopped the car . . . and she started talking.

Extra burdens were added when children tried to make a secret pact with one parent with the plaintive plea 'Please do not tell daddy' or 'Please do not tell mummy'. Some parents immediately refused this request. Others spent days and sometimes weeks obtaining the child's permission to tell other members of the family.

Most families acknowledged that they managed to appear strong in the immediate situation with the child, even though this sometimes involved concealing the enormous surge of anger they felt towards the abuser: 'Inside I felt that I could have killed the man that abused her. Until you experience it, you just don't know what these things do to kids. Seeing the state Gill was in shows you what abuse does to their minds.'

Afterwards, parents who had absorbed children's pain desperately needed to give vent to their feelings to someone else. Foster or adoptive mothers found it brought immense relief to be able to relive the episode with their partner. This reduced the intensity of the experience and at the same time provided them with a more balanced perspective. One adoptive mother vividly portrayed how she had exactly re-enacted the distressed child's antics as she poured the story out to her husband:

'After Mark told me, I was desperate to tell my husband. I was agitated and leaping around squirming. I felt there was a weight inside myself. Everything came out in a total jumble.'

Some families felt strangely implicated in the abuse, even though they knew that they played no part in it: 'You're involved even although you are the innocent party. It gave me an uncomfortable feeling.'

In cases of extreme abuse, it was sometimes hard for family relationships not to be affected:

Sexual abuse carried a different burden . . . You start to feel guilty about going near your own children. You wonder 'How are people interpreting this?' You feel angry at all men. I went through a sticky patch with my husband. I didn't really want anything to do with him. I couldn't bear to touch anyone. Your behaviour becomes 'anti' – the disgust of it. It was a tremendous burden on me.

A number of families commented on the value of writing down a verbatim account of what had happened. This seemed to provide a welcome release of internal tension and also helped families to regain control of their own emotions.

Despite the pain, there was also a very positive element as disclosure created new bonds between parents and children. Feelings of warmth increased towards children who had dared to entrust them with their most personal secret. One adoptive mother related how very special that experience had been for her: 'I felt privileged. I felt that it had been an honour for me to know his secret. After two to three months, he had shared with me what he had kept inside himself for ten years.'

Disclosure opened up a new level of communication. The combination of the fact that parents felt progress had been made, while children demonstrated more amenable behaviour gave a new impetus to the placement. In some situations, it rescued the placement from the brink of disruption.

WHEN DOES DISCLOSURE END?

This study illustrated that there is a sense in which disclosure is never finished. As children grew up, new events, new crises were liable to reawaken painful experiences associated with sexual abuse. This is illustrated in the adoption placement of four-year-old Sharon who had suffered sexual abuse as a toddler. During the early months of placement, Sharon felt able to share her story of abuse with her adopters.

Now Sharon is aged ten. Again and again incidents have occurred which have consciously or subconsciously triggered memories for Sharon from her past. It is helpful to listen to the adoptive mother reminiscing on some of these experiences:

> At five-and-a-half years, Sharon was playing with the girl next door. She started talking to her about babies. Sharon was very upset . . . I was really worried about bringing Sharon's past up again, but I took a deep breath and said 'I think you might be upset because of something that happened to you when you were small'. Then for weeks she wanted to talk everything over again at nights. She said that she was never going to have babies. She was anti boys.
>
> When she was eight years, a girl in Sharon's class started acting sexually in the classroom. She was sticking pencils in her knickers. Sharon felt that it was wrong and became quite hysterical. I used to find her sobbing at the school gate . . . Again, we had to help her through that difficult time . . . and of course there's the future. I often think ahead and ask myself 'Will she be able to love someone after all that has happened to her in the past?'

All adoptive and foster families need to be alert to the fact that sexual abuse is not an experience which can be quickly dealt with and then forgotten. A sensitive awareness and an ability to respond to the ongoing vulnerability of abused children is vital.

CHILDREN WHO ARE UNABLE TO TALK ABOUT THEIR ABUSE

Twenty-six children had been unable to make any type of disclosure to their adoptive or foster family. In five of these placements, families were optimistic that children would yet be able to tell them their personal story. A different outlook surrounded the remaining 21 placements. Some families had clearly never reflected on the positive value of disclosure. Others were convinced that it would be beneficial for children to be able to offload some of their internal distress. However, as placements stretched over months and sometimes years, and children remained tightlipped, they grew increasingly despondent about this ever occurring: 'To Richard it's a secret. He knows that I know his secret. I just wish that he would talk. His outlet is his temper – shouting, swearing and biting. The last thing he will do is tell me what happened.'

Some families sensed that children's staunch loyalty to their own family was the insurmountable barrier blocking disclosure. Others were emphatic that their child needed a much deeper therapy than they could provide.

As families began to talk about whether placements had been rewarding or unrewarding, one salient fact emerged. Placements where children remained silent about their abuse often lacked any sense of fulfilment for adoptive or foster families. On the contrary, dissatisfaction and disillusionment were hallmarks of such placements. Consider the comments of one family who took on an 11-year-old boy whose internal anger about his abuse and abuser was never verbalized. After an exhausting and frustrating placement which terminated before the original six month contract was ended, they gave their verdict: 'We didn't feel that we achieved anything through this placement. He was no better when he left than when he came. We felt that he was too difficult for a family.'

Placements of siblings were particularly interesting. Quite often, one child had talked about abuse, but the other had not managed to do so. Which placement was the more rewarding? Without exception, the one where the child had been able to open up about abusive experiences. The positive and negative sentiments expressed by Bill and Steven's family were typical.

Bill (12) and Steven (10) are brothers. They have been in placement for 11 months. Observe the different attitudes which the foster family display towards each boy:

Bill has talked a whole lot. He had been holding it in. It was a tremendous relief for him to tell. His nightmares stopped. His language was atrocious. He used to say 'Away and suck your cunt' or 'Go and shag yourself. He was constantly trying to shock me. His language has improved 60 per cent. He is more in control of himself and he is putting the past where it ought to be. With Bill, I have seen far more progress than with Steven. He has come on 50 per cent. I'm hoping for 70 per cent.

Steven shows no emotion at all. He has no feeling and no conscience. He is like a shell. It's as if there's no inside to him. Steven would pick up a knife or stool and I would not be sure what he might do with it. His tears and his laugh are false. Everything about him is false. He's a con man. He uses adults for his own advantage. If someone doesn't help Steven, I do not know what he might do. He sees women as sex objects. Women and girls are there to lie on their backs. I don't think that Steven would ever talk to me about his abuse. I've seen far far more progress with Bill than with Steven.

Whether the child was pre-school or school age, there was something about children's inability to communicate about abuse with their foster and adoptive families which added an extra stratum of difficulty and intensity to the placement. Within this type of placement, we see the very worst examples of children going berserk and of completely chaotic behaviour. Children lacked the capacity to control their own instincts and emotions. Frequently, families felt completely out of their depth. Frustrations escalated because it seemed to be so impossible to reach the child on anything other than the most superficial level.

KEY ISSUES RELATED TO DISCLOSURE

Social Workers

Foster and adoptive families require simple practical guidelines about handling disclosure.

The subject of disclosure should be included in training and preparation of substitute families.

It is essential to acknowledge the special difficulties for substitute families associated with communicating about sexual issues with children:
  a) who are of limited intellectual ability;
  b) who perceive sexual abuse as a predominantly positive experience.

Social workers need to invest additional time with families during this crucial period.

It is important to be aware

Foster and Adoptive Families

Even when disclosure occurs prior to placement, children may have additional information to share about abuse after placement.

Signs of sexual abuse are likely to precede language.

Children are likely to talk about physical abuse first. Information about sexual abuse may come later.

It is important not to fall into the trap of making a pact with the child about keeping their disclosure of abuse secret.

Sometimes foster and adoptive families may need to take active steps to help children talk about painful aspects of their abuse, rather than always waiting indefinitely for the that, particularly in cases of extreme abuse, families' own relationships may become distorted.

Social workers are likely to be affected themselves and require appropriate support.

child to take the initiative.

Children may take weeks, months or even years to talk about their abuse. Preconceived ideas about time scales are unhelpful.

Behavioural difficulties are likely to improve as a result of disclosure.

It is important for foster and adoptive families living through disclosure to have someone available on a regular basis who will support them through this difficult period.

6 What if sexual abuse is a factor in the adoptive or foster family's background?

As sexual abuse is more explicitly acknowledged as a problem in our society, more and more adults are revealing that sexual abuse was part of their childhood experiences. Recent studies highlight a wide variation in the estimated number of people in Britain who are likely to have suffered sexual abuse, ranging from 54 per cent[5] to 3 per cent[6]. This means that among the people who apply to foster or adopt children, there are likely to be a proportion of people who have been sexually abused themselves. What are the implications of this for the day-to-day care of abused children?

A degree of perplexity surrounds the question 'Should people who have been sexually abused be accepted as foster or adoptive parents of abused children?' One fear is that their own emotional distress may impede their care of the child. A more serious concern is that such people might themselves become abusers and ultimately subject children to further distressing experiences.

This study included 17 foster or adoptive parents (14 per cent) who acknowledged that they had suffered sexual abuse themselves. Some were happy to talk in detail about the implications of this experience for their fostering or adoption work. Others merely stated the fact that they had been sexually abused, but were reluctant to enlarge on the subject.

One foster carer explained that she had never verbalized her own story of sexual abuse to anyone. She had not thought of the implications of this for her fostering work. Seven years' experience of fostering had brought her into contact with many children from a multiplicity of difficult background situations. When three-year-old Andrew was placed with

[5] NASH, C. L., and WEST, D. J. 'Sexual Molestation of Young Girls' in WEST, D. J. (ed), *Sexual Victimisation*, Gower Press, 1985.
[6] BBC Survey for Childwatch (unpublished).

her in 1988, no one suspected that he had been sexually abused. Suddenly her whole world was thrown into turmoil as Andrew's behaviour led her to suspect that he had been subjected to sexual experiences. One evening, during bath time, Andrew spontaneously announced: 'Grand-dad played with my willy.'

This foster mother faced an enormous dilemma. Major decisions had to be made quickly. One alternative was to bring the placement to an abrupt end. The other was to expose a painful secret which she had kept to herself for years. Gradually she summoned the courage to talk with her social worker about her past and later was able to confide in her husband. Reflecting on her experience, she felt that it was vital for her to be able to talk about her own abuse. In this way, she was able to prevent her strong emotions from overwhelming her and interfering with the placement:

> The whole sexual abuse thing made me feel quite ill. A foster friend said to me 'Don't look after him any more' . . . but he had had such a raw deal already.
>
> I was frightened. I had been abused myself. That made it worse. That was really why I had such a thing about it . . .
>
> I will always be grateful to Andrew – more grateful than he can ever know. Through him, I began to talk about my own abuse for the first time. It gave me an opportunity to open up to my husband about it. In some ways, this placement was the best thing that ever happened to me.

This placement points to the need for all foster and adoptive families to have the opportunity to talk about personal experiences of abuse during the preparation period. The fact that sexual abuse does not appear to be a factor in the child's background at the point of placement is no guarantee that it may not emerge at a later stage when children begin to feel secure enough to talk about their past.

Another foster carer commented: 'If I had not worked through my own abuse, the experience of fostering would have destroyed me.' Talking from personal experience, she went on to delineate the stages which she felt had been essential for her to go through, in order to live with her past while caring for abused children.

a) recognition

This is the stage of believing that sexual abuse has actually taken place. This is likely to involve strong emotions such as anger, fear, distress and a tendency to want to deny the reality of what has occurred because the implications of believing it may be too difficult to tolerate.

b) searching for a personal identity

This is the stage of intense questioning. Key questions in this identity crisis are:
'Who am I?'
'Who was I?'
'Who am I now?'
'Have I changed?'

c) acceptance

This is the stage when the victim of abuse is able to say:
'The abuse should not have happened. It was wrong.'
'It was not my fault.'
'I am able to talk about it because I accept myself.'

It was encouraging to observe how many families who had suffered abuse were able to use some of the most negative experiences in their own lives to help abused children. Individuals who were most highly motivated to help abused children were those who had experienced sexual abuse first hand. One foster carer who had been a victim of abuse herself spent several hours describing the rigours of handling two very aggressive teenage boys. She concluded the interview with the comment:

We've had terrible tantrums. Every door in this house has a hole in it. Furniture has been wrecked. Their clothes have been destroyed. We've gone through three chests of drawers in their bedroom in the past ten months . . . but all the most devastating experiences in the world would not stop me taking another sexually abused child. That is the kind of child whom I have always wanted to help and will go on wanting to help.

Another foster carer had devised her own tools for communicating with abused children. Her ideas originated from her own experience of abuse. By reflecting on her own childhood and considering the kinds of activities which would have helped her to verbalize her 'secret', she developed a fascinating range of original materials.

Some people felt that their own abuse gave them an innate ability to recognize non-verbal cues from children and to convey a unique level of understanding to the child:

I remember how I used to stand staring for days and weeks on end. Everything seemed so distant. I have watched children do exactly the same. I feel that I can understand . . . The child is able to sense that you are a receptacle to absorb their pain.

One adoptive mother talked about some of her most emotional moments with her child: 'I was crying for myself and for her. She realized that I understood. I told her things about my own childhood.'

As abused teenagers fought with so many conflicting emotions and were liable to sink into deep depression, some families tried to inspire hope by referring to their own past and reminding the teenager that survival had been possible: 'I say to Angela "I've been where you were. I've been through it. If I managed to make it, you can". Comparing the two helps.'

Members of foster and adoptive families who had suffered abuse did not themselves escape unscathed. Day-to-day events with the child or unpleasant factors in the child's history could reactivate their own sense of pain. In this way, they were of course vulnerable. This study did illustrate, however, that it was possible for the abused adult and the abused child to interact together in such a way that each was able to benefit from the experience of the other. Children benefited from foster and adoptive families' sensitivity towards their most deep-rooted fears, while carers recognized their own growth as they worked on a daily basis with the child: 'The whole thing reminds you of your own insecurities, but it helps you because you know that you have got over it, and your ongoing care of the child gives you the strength to go on knowing that.'

One way in which foster and adoptive families who had suffered abuse stood out from others in the study was in their overwhelmingly negative attitude towards the abuser. Everyone who took part in the study was asked to comment on their attitude towards the perpetrator. Words like 'angry', 'disgusted', 'shocked' and 'puzzled' were commonly used. Some said they felt 'indifferent' or deliberately tried to 'shut off' their feelings. A number reacted sympathetically. Those families who had suffered abuse often described the same negative feelings but in much stronger terms: 'Angry sounds too light a term to use. The words I really feel could not be repeated. It's sick.'

Their phrases were also noticeably different because they often carried a degree of personal vindictiveness: 'They should be shot'; 'I could have strangled the guy'; 'Deep down I wanted his blood.' Some did not just feel angry and resentful; they felt murderous: 'I just hope for the man's safety that he never dares to turn up on my doorstep. I feel full to the brim with hate and anger. If father ever got access, I would pack my bags and move overnight.'

One adoptive mother felt so strongly about her child's abuser that it was questionable whether she was able to use the child's background material in a way that was helpful for the child. Feelings about her own trauma and the child's history had become too closely interlinked:

I know I have done the wrong thing. The social worker gave me a photograph of Richard's (12 years) mummy and daddy. I will not give it to him because of the abuse. I may let him have it when he is 18 years, but certainly not before that . . . I have refused to work with the parents because of what has happened.

Others who had difficulty containing their feeling felt that the best thing that ever happened to them was having to come face to face with the perpetrator: 'Before I met the abuser, I wanted to kill him. When I met him I had no real feelings at all. My reaction was "Poor thing". I could see that there had been so much destruction in his life and that he desperately needed help.' Another adopter commented: 'When I eventually met father in court, I could not feel angry any more. He seemed a separate person to the person who had abused my child.'

In view of the vital importance of foster and adoptive families being able to help children understand their past and disentangle the conflicting emotions surrounding their abuse, it may be necessary for social workers to invest additional time with carers who have suffered abuse themselves. Disproportionately negative attitudes to the perpetrator are, of course, likely to be transmitted to the child. Some families with an eagerness to help an abused child and with the potential to provide a very special type of parenting because of their own abuse may have a 'blind spot' in this area because vindictive feelings towards their own abuser and the child's abuser may have become subtly interlinked.

The observations contained in this chapter are not to be interpreted as conclusive evidence that abused individuals are always ideal parents for sexually abused children. Clearly each applicant's background situation requires to be examined in detail and the positive and negative features analysed fully. It has, however, been attempted to illustrate through this study that the most vulnerable aspect of some adoptive and foster families' lives may be the very feature which equips them for the task.

KEY ISSUES

Social Workers

The importance of exploring
with all prospective adopters
and foster carers whether
sexual abuse has been a factor
in their background.

Foster and Adoptive Families

The need to be aware that if
sexual abuse has been a factor
in adopters' or foster carers'
own background, painful aspects
are likely to be re-awakened
when caring for an abused child.

7 Day-to-day living with a sexually abused child

Sexual abuse rarely occurred in isolation; it was often one element in a complex history of inadequate and neglectful parenting. Foster and adoptive families faced a multiplicity of sexual, emotional and behavioural problems. Problems commonly associated with deprivation such as eneuresis, encopresis, lying, stealing, attention-seeking, withdrawal and aggression appear again and again throughout the study. It is, of course, an impossible task to establish which difficulties originated from sexual abuse and which could be attributed to other factors. One thing emerged clearly: experienced families felt that parenting a sexually abused child created an unparalleled degree of stress on family life for several reasons:

a) inherent in children's behaviour was an intensity which the families had not previously experienced;
b) the task of caring included a constant monitoring of children's actions to prevent sexual incidents escalating. This exacerbated weariness and exhaustion;
c) there was a sense of isolation associated with being unable to share the weight of the parenting task with a partner. The heaviest burden frequently landed on the shoulders of foster and adoptive mothers, regardless of whether the original perpetrator was male or female.

Undoubtedly, this was a challenging type of parenting. At times, families felt out of their depth as they struggled to handle the intrusion and disruption which abused children brought to their lives. This did not mean that there were no rewards. Most families could talk about positive as well as negative aspects. Even placements which disrupted were not totally bleak experiences. It is important to keep this balance in mind when reading this chapter which focuses so much on problem behaviour.

THE ABUSED CHILD'S INNER TURMOIL

Inconsistent and abusive parenting produced traumatized children. Children's emotions were profoundly affected. Their internal systems had been inappropriately programmed, and it was, therefore, not surprising that they grew up exhibiting emotional responses which were often poorly developed, and sometimes completely haphazard.

The mental, physical and emotional components of the abused child's life were out of harmony. Some children's senses had become so numbed by events that they could not feel pain or identify which part of their body was suffering: 'When Andrew (9) would hit his chin, he thought that the pain was in his tummy. He just did not know where the pain was.' Other children could not release emotion through crying: 'Raymond could not cry. His parents had beaten him up and taunted him: "Don't cry. You're a big boy". He would not cry if he hurt himself.' Sometimes the effect of disclosure on a child like Raymond was like releasing a valve which enabled pent up emotions to escape. Tears flowed for the first time.

Spontaneous responses had often been stifled. Some children developed a permanent but false smile. One foster family, after a year's struggle with a teenage boy, could not hide their disappointment: 'Everything about him is false – his smile – his laugh – his tears.'

There were frustrations associated with abused children being unable to give or receive any form of meaningful affection. Words like 'hollow' and 'empty' were used. Quotations like 'There's no feeling around her' and 'He's like a shell. It's as if there's no inside to him' emphasized the difficulties inherent in this type of parenting.

The experience of trying to make physical contact with Dudley (9) was vividly portrayed by his adoptive father: 'If you tried to cuddle him it was like holding an unresponsive blob. It could have been a cigarette packet.' This particular family derived help by attending a seminar run by Claudia Jewett[7]: 'It was as if Dudley was dead. Claudia Jewett explained that by going through the routine of making him show affection again and again, there was a chance that he might waken up.'

Even though this tactic did not always yield immediate results, there were some indications that in the longer term the amount of energy expended had not been totally in vain: 'I made Dudley send me a birthday card every year, although it meant nothing to him. Now, four years later, he sends me a birthday card with the right emotions.'

[7] JEWETT, CLAUDIA, *Helping Children Cope with Separation and Loss*, Batsford, London, 1982.

Some children's responses were not just frozen but marked by fear. A considerable number recoiled from any form of physical contact. Perseverance was essential if families were to overcome this problem. Some broke through this barrier by looking for simple opportunities to touch the child which were non-threatening. One foster mother commented: 'It is important to try and find a way in when the child moves way. I used to wash one girl's hair every night for several weeks to allow physical contact.' Another tried a different tactic: 'If she cried, I would wipe one tear from her face. I used to pretend "There's a black mark on your face". I would quickly wipe it clean.' In this way, resistances to touch gradually lessened, leaving families pleased that they had not ignored this issue.

TRAPPED BY CONFUSED FEELINGS

Abused children had a very confused view of themselves and of other people around them. Again and again they insisted that they were to blame for events totally outside their control. Any sense of personal pride or worth was often sadly absent. Bleak, dark moods could stretch over days and make a profound impact on family life. Sometimes the child's internal anger would suddenly erupt in a frenzied attack on everything and everybody in close proximity, leaving the most experienced family totally devastated. This section examines how the child's internal confusion manifested itself and affected day-to-day living.

Guilt

Abused children frequently carried a high proportion of guilt: 'Angela would be sitting in the house. A child on the street would fall off her bicycle. She would be convinced that it was her fault.'

Many children were plagued by the thought that the abuse had been their fault. Even very young children were sometimes convinced that they had inflicted pain on their abuser, substantiating this claim by describing how the abuser used to cry during sexual encounters. Some children believed that they deserved a criminal sentence. Others wanted to write one word to their abuser – 'Sorry'. In some situations, a parent who had been actively involved in the abuse died at the point of 'reception into care' or after the placement had occurred. This seemed to add further complications as children fretted about whether their part in the abuse had caused the death.

In one fostering placement where the natural father had been imprisoned for abuse, the mother informed the child that the father had died. Foster and adoptive families had a key role to play in helping children unravel false perceptions and relinquish the high proportion of guilt which they had apportioned to themselves. The fact that abuse was not the child's fault had to be emphasized and re-emphasized. Even after months of work on this theme, families were not always convinced that children had allowed this message to infiltrate their lives.

Low self-image

Children who had been used and abused by adults had a very poor self-image. Many referred to themselves in derogatory terms such as 'naughty', 'bad', 'useless' and 'worthless'. Tears flowed as some complained: 'No one likes me' or 'Nobody wants to be my friend'.

Even children's physical demeanour provided signs of low self-esteem. One boy could not tolerate the thought of looking at himself in the mirror; another would scratch out his face in any photograph; a teenage girl frequently reverted to the foetal position when anything distressed her; others were unable to walk with their head in the air or establish eye contact when talking. One teenager kept asking the question 'Am I mentally handicapped?' In extreme cases, children referred to themselves as animals rather than human beings: 'She used to think that she was a cow. She would lie on the floor making weird noises. She would hunch up on the settee. Her whole upbringing she had been told that she was useless.'

Low self-esteem and self-destructive tendencies in teenagers made them vulnerable to sexual exploitation: 'The biggest thing was explaining to her that she did not have to be used.'

Depression

Even very young children could suffer from deep-rooted depression which pervaded the entire family atmosphere. These bouts could last for days, weeks or even months: 'She went through black closed depressed moods for 18 months. When she was in that state I just had to hold her for hours.'

Solvent abuse created havoc in the lives of some teenagers. Glue sniffing, excessive alcohol consumption and drug abuse created additional turmoil for everyone concerned. Some teenagers made serious suicide attempts. Others tended to revert to the same topic of conversation: 'I want to die.'

In one case where a teenager tried to throw herself from an upstairs bedroom window, the strain on the foster family became so intolerable that they felt compelled to terminate the placement.

Uncontrollable outbursts of anger

Watching children at play could be revealing. The anger and violence expressed could not pass unnoticed. Sometimes it was the quality of play which first alerted families to the traumatic events which had occurred in children's lives:

> I knew there was something wrong. Their games were skeletal and very violent. Joe (5) would make lego into a gun or sword. He was so angry. He would set about Colin (4). Their behaviour was extreme, with shrieks of 'You die', 'I hate you'. They would talk about death, dying and funerals. It was morbid.

At other times, anger was principally directed towards the main carer. This was often the person with whom the child had developed the closest rapport. Anger and violence were strangely interwoven with an extremely possessive attitude: 'All her anger and abuse was directed to me. She would spit, punch, swear, twist my wrist, and throw things at me. She would destroy her clothes and everything in her room. At the same time, she clung to me. She was threatened by others wanting my attention.'

Children frequently attempted to use the same implements in these angry scenes as had been used in their own abuse. Examples included sharp knives, pieces of rope, knitting needles and paper which had been set alight. One 12-year-old boy who behaved very violently towards his adoptive mother was able to tell her that he was doing this 'to pay his parents back' for the way they had abused him.

Sometimes it was as if self-control snapped completely and the child's internal anger was unleashed. These unmanageable episodes were often totally unprovoked by external circumstances and occurred in as many as 22 out of 80 placements:

> Carol (4) had the kind of tantrums I had never encountered before. She would bait me. She spat. She would dip her hands in the spittle and go wild. There was a vindictiveness in her behaviour. She was violent. Everything about her said 'I want to hurt you. You hurt me too, and we will do it to death'. She was like a time bomb. These tantrums could last as long as three-and-a-half to four hours.

Occasionally there was a self-destructive element involved:

> She had a bust up with her father on the phone. She flew at my husband. It took three of us to hold her down. She attacked herself and cut her wrists several times. She used to lie across the hall or kitchen floor. If I went to her, I knew that she would have a go at me. In one of these fits of rage, she swallowed a bottle of anti-depressants. Afterwards she was very repentant.

During some of these eruptions, clothes were torn, bedclothes were ripped apart, bedroom windows were smashed, doors and beds were broken, leaving an entire room in total disarray: 'Suddenly he knocked over a chair. He started screaming and throwing things at me. He broke all the panes of glass in the bedroom window. Everything was completely smashed up. I tried the emergency number. There was no reply. Eventually I dialled 999.'

In several cases, the injuries sustained as a result of these violent scenes needed hospitalization. Some families persevered with the placement despite these onslaughts. Others disrupted following this type of crisis.

SOME EXAMPLES OF DIFFICULT BEHAVIOUR

Constant changes from toddler to adolescent

Children's behaviour was often totally haphazard. One adopter commented: 'It was as if something inside the child was frantically screaming out "Who am I? Who am I?" and nobody could give an answer.' One minute the abused child would behave like a toddler and the next minute like a sophisticated adult with a repertoire of flirtatious behaviour. These constant fluctuations tested some families' patience to the limit.

One adoptive mother vividly portrayed her 12-year-old boy moving like a whirlwind from one activity to another. She smiled as she explained how her social workers had emphasized how essential it was to reinforce his good behaviour by praising him:

> His behaviour was all jumbled up together. It was just one big mess. For five minutes, he would act like a two-year-old – then he would change to a four-year-old – then back to two years. Then he would be this older boy who was trying to be sensible. On the whole, if he was good, it was usually for no longer than five minutes.
>
> My social worker would say 'You must find chances to praise him' –

but he's roused you to so much anger and frustration because you feel so powerless. Suddenly he is good for a little while – but because my emotions are of anger and frustration, how can you turn it to being nice and say 'Well done'? You just can't change that quick – and before you know what is happening, the moment is lost and he has gone off at another tangent.

Another family who had been fostering a four-year-old girl for six months felt totally overwhelmed by the child's disordered behaviour. They reached the decision to terminate the placement unless they could find a constructive way of handling these disturbed behaviour patterns. Advice from a child psychologist was the key to the survival of this placement:

> She explained that when she was being a one-year-old, I should let her be a one-year-old for five minutes and then bring her back. If she wanted to be a teenager, that I should let her be a big girl for a few minutes. Even today (one year later), if she gets upset I will let her be a two-year-old for a few minutes and then say 'Can I have Cheryl back now as a six-year-old?'

Obsessional traits

The personal items which some teenagers hoarded seemed to have a sexual connotation. These included sanitary towels and underwear. Some were fastidious about personal hygiene, washing and re-washing any article of clothing which had touched their body. One girl bought new pants every day and changed about 15 times daily. Washing and bathing were problematic for children who were frightened of touching their own bodies or letting anyone else do so. Boys in particular were often preoccupied with their bodily functions, constantly brooding on the thought that their sex organs were abnormal or had been damaged through sexual activity.

Self-mutilation

Self-mutilation was a very difficult habit to break. Arms and legs were scratched and cut with sharp knives, keys, razor blades and a school compass; fingers were bitten to the point of bleeding; scars which were in the process of healing were re-opened; lips and cheeks were so badly bitten that they were sometimes permanently disfigured.

Some children seemed to display destructive tendencies towards their sex organs. Several boys masturbated to the point of causing bleeding and requiring hospitalization; another boy had distorted the shape of his penis; while a teenager was attending hospital because he had completely destroyed one of his testicles.

Eneuresis/encopresis

Eneuresis was a common problem affecting all age groups. Some children urinated everywhere, including on walls, carpets and bed-clothes; bedwetting occurred frequently. In one case, a four-year-old girl attempted to drink her own urine. Soiling was much less common. In a smaller number of cases, soiling and smearing occurred. Sometimes articles of clothing which had been soiled with faeces were deliberately hidden among other family members' belongings.

THE INTRUSIVE ELEMENT

Abused children invaded family life, unsettling established roles and relationships and sapping away the energies of those caring for them. Foster and adoptive parents were especially vulnerable as their tolerance level was often stretched to its ultimate level. Several admitted that it was virtually impossible to estimate in advance how heavy the personal toll would be of caring for an abused child.

Sapping the family's emotional space and energy

Sometimes an abused child took exclusive possession of one adult in the family, blocking everyone else's access to that person. Hostility and jealousy soon became all pervasive:

> She was so clingy to my husband. Whenever he walked in the door from work, she would be hanging round his legs. She was so possessive. Was it because she lacked a father figure, or was she trying to make him sexually aroused? If he went to the toilet she would be sitting outside the toilet waiting for him.

Children had the ability to exhaust all the emotional space in an adult's life. In particular, adoptive and foster mothers complained of feeling 'smothered', 'suffocated' and 'trapped' as children invaded their private space: 'He used to walk along the road squashed against me. He was trying to be part of me. It was unbearable. He was trying to get inside me.' Others complained of children 'walking on their heels', or 'wanting to get inside their shoes' or of 'tripping them up' as they walked along the road.

Inside the home, these feelings of claustrophobia were even more difficult to tolerate. Some felt compelled to remove themselves from the same room as the abused child. Others waited until the child was in bed before making their escape:

> I used to feel that the four walls were closing in on me. At night, I used to go out in the car and drive around aimlessly. She had invaded all my space. I used to joke to my husband 'I wish that someone would find me a family. I wish that someone would take me into care'.

The battle for control

Children who had been treated as adults on a sexual level in their own families had great difficulty accepting their position as a child in adoptive and foster families. They were constantly battling for adult status. Abused children were described as 'dominant', 'controlling' and 'powerful'. In single-parent families, the role of mother came under threat: 'She doesn't realize adults are in control. She dominates. She's a much better mother than me. She would take over the younger children completely.'

In other families, attempts were made to usurp the position of wife and mother. Behaviour was often flirtatious: 'She demolished women. She wanted to take over the mother/power role. She's a very powerful sexualized girl.'

Some boys tried to aspire to being the 'perfect' husband: 'When my husband was away, Tom (12) would say "Are you missing dad? I could take dad's place. I could be romantic." He would ask me about my sexual behaviour. He wanted to control me. He would order me around.'

Children touched the central nerve of family life. Assumptions about roles and status in families were thrown into disarray. Individual family members seethed with anger as their position in the family was threatened, and yet they were often too embarrassed to admit that a child could evoke such sensitive feelings inside them. These difficulties were not restricted to the early weeks and months of placement when adjustments were essential for everyone. Some of these problems still undermined placements which had stretched over a number of years, giving them an uncertain and unsteady quality.

A CLOSER EXAMINATION OF THE SEXUAL ELEMENT AND ITS IMPACT ON FAMILY LIFE

Children's histories of sexual abuse evoked strong reactions for some foster and adoptive families. In rare cases, cuddling, holding or comforting the child became problematical for the carer because of the revulsion felt towards the abuser and towards the fact that children's bodies had been violated. A few reported that the child's flesh was 'creepy' or even 'repugnant'. These emotions had to be overcome if the placement was to succeed.

Even the physical space which the child occupied in the family could take on negative connotations. One foster mother acknowledged how uncomfortable she felt when she approached the abused teenager's bedroom:

> She moved into a bedroom which had been occupied by my ten-year-old son. It had been a very nice homely room . . . She used to write obscene words on the wall. I used to hate going into it. It had such a powerful, hateful, hostile feeling. It made me feel that I was not welcome there.

Handling sexualized behaviour

Figure 7 Display of sexualized behaviour

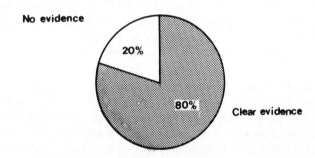

Although sexualized behaviour was a common problem, it was not an automatic feature in every sexual abuse case. In a small proportion, only 16 out of 80 placements (20 per cent), no overt sexual acts were exhibited by abused children. A closer examination indicates that this figure was probably an overestimate: within the group of 16 placements were three where serious doubts existed about whether sexual abuse was an accurate

71

diagnosis. In another placement which had only lasted for three days, there was inadequate time for sexualized behaviour to exhibit itself. Four children developed the opposite approach. They retreated from any type of physical contact, displayed fear of their own bodies, disliked their developing sexuality and had an instinctive aversion to anything sexual. Although these children's behaviour patterns presented less embarrassment within a social context, the experience of sexual abuse had left definite scars in their lives also.

Sexual overtures from abused children included a range of behaviour from touching the foster or adoptive parents' genital areas, through to demands for sexual intercourse. These overtures were often reserved for one rather than both adults in the family. There did not seem to be any definite pattern about which parent was approached sexually. For example, it did not automatically follow that children would act sexually towards the parent of the same sex as their abuser. One highly experienced carer commenting on sexual episodes with a ten-year-old foster boy suggested that the gender of the parent was immaterial: 'He was sitting opposite me flirting with me. I don't think that it would have mattered too much if I had been the dog or the cat. He had been sexually abused by his father, who was the main carer. OK – I was female – but I was still the main carer.'

It was not unusual for the same parent who was receiving sexual overtures to be simultaneously experiencing rejection by the child. The form the rejection took varied from case to case. It could be a blanket refusal to communicate, a fretful withdrawal, or a more aggressive approach which included physical attacks. The fact that this parent often had no rapport with the child other than that based on the child seeking a sexual relationship made it exceptionally difficult for the family to know exactly how to respond.

Even very young children were capable of pronounced sexualized behaviour. Patricia was aged only three, but her behaviour had clear sexual overtones: 'Patricia was so disturbed at night. She would waken in the middle of the night to masturbate. She would lie on the bed with her legs wide apart. It was an obvious invitation to me to "come on".'

Just occasionally, a foster or adoptive parent provided some useful insights into how difficult the experience of sexual touching had been for them. Perhaps because more interviews were completed with women than with men, it came up more frequently with foster and adoptive mothers. A number of women felt strongly that it was an issue which literature on sexual abuse had failed to address. Families who had participated in training courses felt that it was a glaring omission from these programmes also: 'Courses talk about men protecting themselves. Why do they never talk about the mum? It was the most creepy thing that I ever experienced. Nobody prepared me for that.'

Similar sentiments were echoed in other interviews: 'He touched the top of my breast. My blood ran cold. I could feel the imprint of his hand for hours afterwards. I felt like I was being abused.' Adults were not indifferent to children's sexual overtures. At least one adoptive father acknowledged during the course of the interview that touching had the effect of making him feel sexually aroused. Another single adopter surprised herself by her reaction:

> I used to be puzzled about how a mother could sexually abuse her son – but the whole thing has created problems in me. A lot of what David has been saying and doing has stirred me up. I had not expected that. It has awakened my own sexual needs as a female. It is something that I have not really resolved – and it took me completely by surprise.

Children who had been treated as sexual partners in their own home environment had been conditioned to expect an identical pattern when they joined their foster or adoptive family:

> Shortly after they came, our own girls went to grandma's for the weekend. Our foster girls Amy (7) and Emma (4) went frantic. I could not get them to go to bed. In the end, it turned out that they assumed that my husband usually went to bed with our girls and as they were away, they thought 'It'll be us tonight'.

Some children had developed the technique of using their bodies sexually to gain favour with their abuser. Now they were replicating these patterns of behaviour with their foster and adoptive families and were confused to discover that they were unable to achieve the same results. In the following example, a foster mother describes how a 12-year-old girl behaved towards her after a family row.

> One of the girls had a horrific tantrum. She was threatening to throw herself out of the window. She stormed upstairs shouting a load of abuse. At 6 p.m. she appeared on the stairway in the most revealing nightie. She started crawling downstairs face forward on her stomach. She had her face up towards me. Everything about her was provocative. She put her hands on my legs and started to sidle up my legs. It was her way of saying 'Sorry'. It was learned behaviour.

There was immense confusion in some children's minds about the roles of individuals in the family. The case of 12-year-old Tim vividly portrays this. Tim's father died when he was seven years old. Since his father's death, his mother had used him as her regular sexual partner. Consequently, sexual activity between mother and son had become the norm for Tim. A high degree of patience and understanding was essential as Tim brought his own skewed interpretation of relationships into his new family:

> He asks me if I love him, why can I not show it in a physical way. He wants sex. To him that's what mums and sons do. He needs cuddling. The problem is how to allow him the contact he needs and where to draw the line.
>
> When he approaches me suggestively, I reject him. I used to say to him 'You're approaching me the wrong way'. He had no idea what I meant and he used to get so frustrated.

Some children had been involved in a three-way sexual relationship with their parents. This frequently involved the child being taken into bed with both parents when sexual intercourse occurred, and being forced to participate in the sexual act. Eight-year-old Susan had experienced this type of family lifestyle. When she was placed for adoption with John and Mary Smith, she immediately tried to instigate the same type of sexual behaviour with her new family. Whenever any physical contact occurred between John and Mary, Susan quickly imitated this behaviour. For example, if Mary sat on John's knee, as soon as she got off, Susan would jump on and want to receive the same warm caresses from John. The Smith family found this an exceptionally difficult situation to manage. Privately, Mary seethed with anger, but she did not find it easy to admit to anyone just how jealous she felt. On the other hand, John felt sorry for Susan because she had missed out on so much physical attention. Denying Susan this type of warm physical contact was in his mind equated with failing to meet one of the child's most basic needs. In some placements, these situations ignited all sorts of unexpected emotional responses and could only too easily escalate to crisis proportions.

Susan's case is just one example of how adept children were at creating rifts between adults. A much larger number could be cited. In one placement where the parents separated and the placement disrupted, the adoptive father did not conceal the fact that the stresses of the placement had contributed to divorce proceedings. In other placements, families readily acknowledged how divisive the child's behaviour had been:

> She tried to drive a wedge between us. She used to use me as a weapon against my husband. She would skirt around him looking for a

reaction. He found it difficult. She thought that she was an adult. She was trying to compete for a higher place in the family than a child.

DAY-TO-DAY DILEMMAS ASSOCIATED WITH THE CHILD'S SEXUALIZED BEHAVIOUR

Is regression appropriate or inappropriate for a sexually abused child?

Many children had missed out on any positive parenting in the early months and years of their lives. One way of trying to compensate for those missing experiences was by letting children regress through baby and toddler stages of development. This posed special problems in relation to children who had suffered sexual abuse, because in their experience any form of physical closeness had usually entailed sexual contact. Consequently, some experienced families who had felt comfortable about allowing other 'hard to place' children to regress were often too frightened to work in a similar manner with the abused child. Primarily, they feared that the sexual element would get out of control. A small group of families were brave enough to tackle this. All described positive outcomes for the child. At each stage, they found it essential to set clear boundaries in relation to physical contact for themselves and the child.

One adopter described how 12-year-old Simon demonstrated a clear need to regress. Taking her cue from the child, she succeeded in bringing him back through infant phases of development. The fact that Simon was exhibiting very sexualized behaviour did not deter her. Looking back, she had no doubts about the value of this experience for Simon:

> The social worker said that regression was a positive sign, so I was looking for it. Three to four months after Simon came, a baby dropped a dummy on a bus. Simon asked if he could take it home and suck it. I said that I would buy him one. I bought him a baby's bottle. One evening I came downstairs and offered it to him. He was thrilled. I would fill it with fruit juice for him and he would suck it. I think he used it for about two to three weeks.
>
> A few weeks later, when I was talking to him about his birth mum, he said that she had never put a nappy on him. He wanted to wear a nappy. I cut up pieces of sheet to simulate nappies. He would wear his nappy in the evenings. He worried about what might happen if he wet it, so I had to give him my full permission to wet it. He wore the nappy

for several weeks. One evening, he came downstairs with a nappy in his hand. He wet one corner of it. That seemed to be important to him because that marked the end of the nappy phase. I asked him last week if he remembered wearing nappies last year. He had absolutely no recollection of it.

More recently, he has wanted to curl up in the foetal position. He will curl up beside me on the living room settee as if he is inside my tummy. I tell him to relax and to think that he is actually inside me. He needs that kind of security because there have been so many holes in his life.

These phases have led to progress. It has been a way of filling up some of the insecurities in his past. It has been a type of healing for him. His childhood was so back to front. He had no foundation on which to build. He needed to experience his childhood the right way round. If we had not gone through these phases, it would have been like trying to build for the future when there was nothing to build on – just a foundation of holes.

When asked if regression had triggered any sexualized behaviour, this adopter gave an interesting response:

I could clearly distinguish when Simon was being a baby or a toddler and when he was being a 12-year-old. The atmosphere was completely different . . . There were other times when he was behaving very sexually and asking 'why can I not have sex with you?' The mood had changed. It was at these times that I had to draw the line with him.

Commenting on her experiences of allowing Simon to regress, this adoptive mother stressed the following key points:

a) the importance of taking her cue from the child. Simon clearly demonstrated when he wanted to regress and how he wanted to regress;
b) Simon clearly set time limits for each phase. He indicated when the phase was complete;
c) the importance of having a knowledgeable professional to consult during this period. In this case, the social worker was available to advise and encourage the family.

The dilemma of establishing normal physical contact with the abused child

The fact that the abused child could so easily misinterpret any form of physical contact as a cue for sexual contact had enormous implications for day-to-day living. If the child had been sexually abused by a male, social workers were prone to advise the foster or adoptive father to keep the child at arm's length. It became apparent during a number of interviews that some fathers had become so frightened that they were detaching themselves almost completely from the abused child. In these situations, all overtures of affection from the abused child were being quickly spurned by the foster or adoptive father, but of course they continued to respond in an active manner to their own children. At best, this approach seemed to achieve nothing beneficial for the abused child. At worst, it is possible that the abused child interpreted these rebuffs as further rejection, especially when they were being treated so differently from other children in the family.

Other foster and adoptive families took a more helpful approach by showing the child how to be physically close without being sexually close, by drawing clear boundaries in relation to physical contact between themselves and the child, and by teaching the child rudimentary facts about appropriate and inappropriate relationships. This was, of course, a difficult task. From the adults' point of view, it was easier to keep the child at a distance rather than working through these problems stage by stage.

Two facts emerge clearly from this study:

a) social workers need to be clearer about how the physical and emotional needs of sexually abused children can be met through substitute families.
b) families need help and direction if they are to respond effectively to abused children's need for physical contact at the same time as re-educating the child about the essential difference between physical contact and sexual contact.

DISRUPTIONS

Ten out of 80 placements had disrupted and an additional placement was on the brink of breakdown. Three were adoption placements, although none had actually reached the stage of finalized adoption Eight placements disrupted because of the child's uncontrollable and chaotic behaviour, resulting in violent and dramatic temper tantrums. In these situations, families frequently made valiant and prolonged efforts to withstand the most devastating onslaughts of physical and verbal abuse, often resulting in considerable damage to the contents of their home; eventually, however, the ultimate crisis occurred. Disruption left a trail of hurt, guilt, relief and sometimes exasperation as the family felt disappointed that they had been unable to penetrate the child's deepest problems. Some reached the conclusion that the child was 'unplaceable'; others expressed the viewpoint that the placement might work in the future if an effective therapeutic service could be offered to the child in the intervening period.

One significant factor could not pass unnoticed. The eight children whose placements disrupted due to uncontrollable behaviour had another feature in common: they were all unable to share the intimate details of their abuse with their foster or adoptive parents. It seemed that if children could not give vent to their story of abuse by using language, internal tensions burst out in all directions. Conversely, talking about abuse seemed to help children to calm down and gain a measure of self-control. A clearer picture of this connection emerges by charting and comparing the development of cases where children were able and unable to talk about their abuse.

Children unable to talk about abuse within the foster/ adoptive family	Children able to talk about abuse within the foster/ adoptive family
Children seemed unable to control internal tensions. Behaviour became more and more chaotic and less controllable.	Behavioural problems lessened. The frequency and intensity of violent episodes reduced as children seemed to be more in control of themselves.
Family felt frustrated in their endeavour to help the child and consequently less fulfilled in their parenting role.	Family felt encouraged and even honoured that the child had been able to share such an intimate aspect with them. Consequently, they experienced a closer bond between themselves and the child as a result of disclosure.
The fact that the bond between family and abused child was weak and the parents' level of fatigue was high made the placement vulnerable.	The combination of these two positive factors strengthened the family's ability, determination and commitment to persevere with the placement.

Referring to the importance of children being able to disclose, one experienced foster carer commented: 'As long as the abused child finds someone to confide in about what has happened, it doesn't really matter who it is. It could be a therapist, social worker or teacher.'

The majority of families who took part in this study, however, were not in total agreement with this theory. They felt that it was children's ability to disclose to them in particular which made the most crucial difference to whether children were able to integrate into the family. In their opinion, the fact that children were able to talk about abuse with a therapist or another professional person did not seem to produce the same degree of change or have any significant bearing on the bonding process within the substitute family.

In view of the small number of disruptions studied, it would be unrealistic to make a categorical statement about a correlation between children's inability to disclose and disruption. A larger study is clearly essential in order to substantiate this claim. These indicators have major implications for the following aspects of adoption and fostering practice:

a) ensuring that disclosure work is defined as a priority area in placement work of sexually abused children;
b) ensuring that foster and adoptive families receive relevant preparation and support to enable them to undertake this critical aspect of the work effectively.

REWARDS

After identifying such a long list of difficulties, the question arises 'Were there any rewards?' Eight out of 66 families (12 per cent) searched for something positive to say. Regrettably, they had to acknowledge that there had been no rewards for them. The remaining 58 families perceived the experience rather differently. They had no difficulty describing rewarding aspects, although they never pretended that the task was easy. One adopter commented: 'I would say that the ratio of reward to effort was 10 to 90. For us, it was like a nuclear bomb that exploded.' Another experienced foster carer sighed as she offered her verdict: 'You have to expect to give a lot of yourself and not get a lot back.'

New adopters in particular acknowledged that their original expectations had sometimes been totally unrealistic. Initial words of warning from their social worker had passed unheeded. Even in cases like this, where the most radical adjustments had to be made, enthusiasm and an unswerving commitment towards the child were striking features.

At the beginning, our social worker used to say to us 'It's going to be hard'. We used to laugh. We were expecting instant change – but we have had to learn that it doesn't work that way. We will keep going now. No matter what happens, we will stick with it. We feel good. We know that we have been able to help the children.

Families did observe progress. Robot-like behaviour altered; children became more relaxed, confident and happier. Occasionally, these changes were quite startling: 'It has been amazing to watch a battered, bruised and frail child change from a trembling wreck into a bright, bubbly child with so much to offer life.' Behaviour improved too, and families could not deny that they had given children hope for the future.

Some families, contemplating the fact that they had rescued a child from an abusive situation were inspired to press on. Others thrived on the challenging nature of the work. One adopter who had tackled a very explosive placement felt that she had found her niche in life: 'It has made me feel a lot better about myself. It has given me a purpose in life. Before I did this, there seemed to be something missing. Mark has made up for that. We don't regret it. He means so much to us.'

Individuals who had been victims of sexual abuse themselves went a step further: 'I feel totally fulfilled. I could cry trying to explain it to you. Just seeing the child's look of fear and shame turn to normality makes it all worthwhile.' Perhaps the clearest indicator that there were rewards was the fact that as many as 46 out of 66 families (70 per cent) stated that they would have no hesitation in taking on another sexually abused child if this opportunity became available in the future.

SUMMARY OF DIFFICULTIES EVIDENCED IN STUDY

0–5 years	5–11 years	11–18 years
Bedwetting/urinating everywhere.	Urinating everywhere.	Bedwetting/urinating everywhere.
Soiling/smearing.	Soiling.	Soiling/smearing.
Temper tantrums.	Aggressive play.	Violent tantrums/complete wrecking of room.
Chronic nightmares/disturbed sleep patterns.	Violent tantrums.	Maltreating animals.
Periods of deep depression.	Nightmares (sexual connotations).	Aversion to foods (runny eggs). *
Inability to play.	Aversion to food (salad cream). *	Excessive masturbation (hiding the evidence).
Aggressive play (monsters/death/dying).	Emotionless: unable to cry or feel pain.	No idea of privacy or sex boundaries.
Aversion to foods (blancmange, Instant Whip – anything that reminds child of semen). *	Jealous of adoptive father.	Preoccupied with whether sex organs function normally.
Self abusive (picking fingers, cutting legs, clawing face).	Exposing genital areas.	Fear of developing sexuality or sexual relationship.
	Masturbation to the point of bleeding.	Sleeping with clothes on.

0–5 years	5–11 years	11–18 years
Fear of foster/adoptive father.	Fear of bedtime. with adoptive mother. Walking along road squashed against adoptive mother (trying to get inside her).	Requesting sexual intercourse
Excessive masturbation.		Women perceived as sex objects.
Rigid when changing nappy.	Continual sexual remarks.	Sexual activity with sibling.
Refusing to touch genitals.	Asking strangers personal details of their sex life.	Asking strangers 'Have you had sex today?'
Terrified of rough and tumble games or any physical contact.	Wanting to show off pubic hair to strangers.	Behaving sexually inside and outside the family.
Fear of foster father washing or bathing.	Telling everyone about sexual abuse.	Sexual allegations against foster father.
Kissing open mouthed.	Vulnerable in bedroom.	Promiscuity.
Fondling breasts (foster mother or stranger).	Frightened of any close physical contact.	Solvent abuse (glue, alcohol and drugs).
Sexual play with other children.	Refusal to remove underpants when having a bath.	Self mutilation (carving and re-opening scars).
Dominance.	Touching/lying on top of other children sexually.	Obsessional about cleanliness and tidiness.
Fluctuations in behaviour from toddler to sophisticated teenager.	Touching parents or strangers.	Domineering.

0–5 years	5–11 years	11–18 years
	Requesting sexual intercourse.	Rejecting adoptive father.
	Accusing other children of touching.	Depression.
	Offering another child money for sex.	Hoarding sanitary towels.
	Lying.	Feigning illness.
	Stealing.	School refusal.
	Absconding.	Inability to make friends.
	Inability to make meaningful friendships with peers.	

★ Relevant to children who had been involved in oral sex.

Note:

All these difficulties are not necessarily attributable to sexual abuse. It is important to remember that most children in the study had not only been sexually abused; many had also suffered other forms of emotional and physical abuse.

8 The impact on other children in the family

Sixty-nine out of 80 placements (86 per cent) were made with families who already had other children ranging in age from young babies to adolescents. There was no definite pattern associated with the place the sexually abused child occupied in the family. Twenty-three children were placed as the youngest family member, and eight as the eldest. Some families were large, comprising foster, adoptive and step-children. A few families had one or more children with disabilities. Occasionally, a sexually abused child was very close in age to another child in the family. Some foster families cared for several sexually abused children simultaneously.

Most families made some attempt to prepare the other children in a general way for the arrival of a new foster or adoptive child. Very few made any effort in advance of the placement to talk with their children about the sexual abuse aspect and how this might affect them. Some felt that it would be unfair on the new child to do this. Others were concerned about instigating prejudice or fear. At times, it seemed premature to talk about facts which might later be disproved. The most common approach was for parents to make a general comment to their children like: 'If X does anything unusual, let us know immediately.' With this note of caution underpinning the placement, parents approached the task with their eyes and ears open. They were ready to intervene if anything of an inappropriate sexual nature began to affect their children.

There was clear evidence that bringing a sexually abused child into the family placed the other children in a vulnerable situation, especially when they were not adequately forewarned about potential difficulties. With hindsight, some families felt that they had made a mistake by not talking with their own children from the outset. One family who fostered a 12-year-old girl made a conscious decision not to talk with their teenage boys about the sexual abuse aspect of the case. Privately they reasoned:

'A 12-year old girl would never want to confide in adolescent boys on such an intimate subject.' Within days of the placement, they were proved completely wrong. They learned by hard experience that this is an area of work where assumptions can easily be misguided. This family resolved that they would include their boys more fully in all future placements.

However attuned parents were to their own children's needs, sexually abused children often exerted an influence before parents had time to intervene. Occasionally, abused children decided to tell their story to a child in the family rather than an adult. There were instances of children as young as two-and-a-half being involved in this way. In another case, a boy of four disclosed unexpectedly to his foster family late one evening after all the other children had gone to bed. The next morning, as soon as he was awake, he rushed into their eight-year-old girl's bedroom. While she was getting ready for school, he poured out his entire story to her. Naturally, she was startled. She had never heard anyone talk like this before. Her parents were themselves still recovering from the shock of the disclosure which had occurred less than 24 hours previously and they had not had adequate time to do the groundwork with their daughter.

Sometimes one of the children in the family happened to be present when a disclosure was made to an adult. This happened to Kerry (10), who suffered from cerebral palsy. By chance, she was in the bedroom with her mother when her four-year-old adoptive brother Karl started to talk about his abuse for the first time. Karl expressed anger, bitterness and resentment. With his adoptive mother pinned to the wall, he began hitting and biting her as his disjointed story slowly emerged. Looking on, Kerry feared that her mother would be injured. She found it difficult to understand the complex dynamics of this emotional scene. In this situation, Kerry's mother not only had to cope with Karl's distress, but also had to produce simple explanations to pacify her daughter.

Sexually abused children brought an increased awareness of sexual issues into the family. Some families talked about their children's 'innocence being destroyed' as they listened to lurid stories of abuse. Parents could not totally control the verbal and non-verbal signals which their children were exposed to: 'They were totally obsessed with lovers and willies. They were always drawing pictures of willies. They were so crude with the girls. They were always trying to shock them.'

Of course, some abused children were expert at gaining other children's attention as they explained the facts of life in explicit detail. At least one toddler was mystified as he rushed to check out the facts with his foster family: 'Shaun was two years. He came running to me one day

Figure 8 Placements where sexual activity occurred with other children

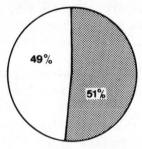

"Lyn said that her daddy hurt her with his pink stick on the bottom. Her daddy wouldn't do that. Daddies don't do that, do they?"'

The impact of sexual abuse on other children was not merely confined to verbal communication: in 35 out of 69 placements (51 per cent), some type of sexual activity was directed towards another child in the family. This included a wide range of behaviour from sexually abused children kissing other children open mouthed; peering at them in the toilet; being obsessed with a baby's genitals; sexual play; touching; clawing; lying on top of other children sexually; inappropriate displaying of body; removing their own and other children's underclothes. Some parents were troubled with nagging doubts about the likelihood of these incidents escalating into more serious sexual episodes. Others worried that their children might enjoy the experience and want to imitate it with their peers. However, there was no indication of these fears being realized.

Such events and incidents spurred families into action. A number used these opportunities to gather all the children around them and to teach them the rudimentary facts about relationships. Books on 'good' and 'bad' touching were useful aides. Many families perceived these events as having positive rather than negative results because they forced a new openness about sexual issues among all family members and opened up a quality of communication which had not previously been possible.

Certain groups of children were especially vulnerable. Children with disabilities were often singled out as targets for sexual advances. Generally, they were good at safeguarding themselves; even if they had inadequate speech, they were usually able to scream. Some families worried about babies who were too young to protect themselves. A number stated that they would never leave a baby alone with the abused child or relax their watchfulness, even for a few minutes: 'She would want to change the shittiest nappy, and at the first opportunity she would strip the baby off. She was obsessed with small children's private parts. She just could not be trusted.'

There were extra risks associated with placing a number of sexually abused children together in the same family. When two children who had very sexualized lifestyles were placed in close proximity, a powerful sexual dynamic could be at work. In some instances, foster children did manage to engage together sexually, causing endless distress for the foster family:

> I found Aaron (8 years) in bed with another six-year-old foster child. He said that he was trying to 'screw' her. I asked the professionals 'Can children have intercourse?' The answer I got was 'We don't know'. All they could say was that she could not get pregnant.

There were also positive aspects associated with placing several abused children in the same family. One child talking about abuse helped to break the ice for others. Feelings of isolation were reduced. When a crisis erupted with one abused child, it often helped to bring sensitive issues out into the open for other foster children. Some foster families admitted that they found it much easier to work collectively with a group of abused children rather than with an individual child. The group itself provided an immediate and spontaneous therapeutic situation.

Sibling placements brought some additional complexities to family life. The study included 14 sibling placements; in eight of these placements, some type of sexual activity occurred between siblings. This included siblings masturbating together or trying to engage in sexual intercourse. Siblings often engaged together sexually in the most blatant and open manner, regardless of whether they had an audience or not. This phenomenon inevitably involved other children as they witnessed these strange encounters and sometimes wanted to imitate them. These behaviour patterns were often difficult to break, because they had been learned over prolonged periods. Practical steps had to be devised to monitor sibling relationships. Attempts were made to educate and re-educate them about relationships. In one case where gross abuse had occurred, the foster family had to resort to a more drastic remedy:

> I suspected that Kath (11) and Raymond (14) had had sex before. There were all the tell-tale signs. They always sat so close together. I never left them alone together. At night, I installed baby alarms and I had two way radios in each room. I had to monitor things. Several times I stopped them . . . I used the alarms for 18 months and then I removed them.

All siblings did not engage in overt or covert sexual behaviour. Some adopted exactly the opposite approach as one tried to protect the other from any risk of sexual exploitation. The most simple family activity could trigger feelings of alarm and cause an over-anxious brother or sister to intervene: 'My husband was playing a game of chasing with two-and-a-half year old May. Her six-year-old sister started to get upset. She lifted May's skirt. Then she said "She'll be OK. She's got her knickers on." '

Sometimes the impact on other children in the family did not originate from direct contact with the abused child, but rather as a result of foster and adoptive parents' own attitudes to sexual malpractice. Faced with the reality of sexual abuse, some parents reacted with horror. In one case where the foster children had been subjected to all kinds of sexual practices, the foster mother faced an internal struggle; she retreated from touching anyone in the family, including her own children. Touch became associated with guilt, fear and disgust. Anger, confusion and disillusionment became powerful sentiments, threatening to overwhelm her everyday living. She could not prevent herself from feeling strangely implicated in the foster children's abuse. This type of major reaction was not common. When it did occur, it was a temporary phase of difficulty rather than something which permanently affected the family.

Despite the degree of sexualized behaviour exhibited in families, sexual issues were by no means the ones which had the most profound impact on the other children. A much more crucial issue was the fact that the abused child often absorbed so much parental time and energy that inevitably other children felt they were being pushed aside. A number of families described their own sense of weariness associated with the abused child's craving for attention and affection. These demands were exacerbated by the need to supervise all the abused child's activities to ensure that sexualized incidents did not escalate and to protect everyone from the risk of allegations of sexual abuse:

When it's a question of sexual abuse, it wears you down. When I read the diary, I just don't know how we coped. Emotionally and physically, it wears you down. You have to have your attention on them every minute of the day. They want attention immediately. If you don't give it, they could harm one of the other children to get attention. It's a constant worry. The child teaches your own child new 'games'. It is so difficult to explain to my son why it happens. After all, he's only five. You have to try and keep on top of things all the time and watch, watch, watch.

Adoptive and foster parents often felt guilty because a disproportic
amount of time had to be lavished on the abused child. They were
first to acknowledge that it was hard for them to divide themselves ev
between all their children. Some made no secret of the fact that
practical outcome of parenting a sexually abused child was that t
other children inevitably missed out on their attention and affectioi

Some abused children were so damaged that it was hard for then
engage in normal reciprocal relationships with other children in
family. Sometimes abused children were so preoccupied with themsel
that they stood aloof from other children while simultaneously attach
themselves like limpets to adults in the family. Rivalries occurred
these situations as other children found themselves forced to fight
ensure that they received adequate parental recognition.

Sexually abused children were also adept at driving wedges in fam
relationships. This extended to any relationship which was worki
satisfactorily, including relationships between parents and children. O
single parent dissolved into tears as she described how the demands
the placement had brought her seriously to consider disruption:

> Carolyn (13) drives a wedge between me and the other children. Sl
> takes up so much time. Her whole being consumes the entire famil
> She's like a 27-year-old infant. It's so tiring, and there's no escape.
> have thought of disruption, but for Carolyn that would be horrendou:
> She's put all her eggs in one basket, and this is her basket.

Sometimes other children did not like the abused child. This was usuall
in cases where the abused child's behaviour was disruptive or wher
spiteful incidents occurred such as faeces being smeared on othe
children's toys or clothes, or soiled underpants being planted amon;
another child's belongings. Occasionally, the abused child had difficulty
understanding about boundaries in family relationships. Some teenagers
seethed because their privacy was invaded. One foster mother was
adamant that the issue of space should be a very crucial consideration for
any family contemplating taking on this work. She felt that it was vital for
other children in the family to have adequate space to carry on their own
interests and activities without constantly feeling smothered by the
presence of the abused child.

Disruptive behaviour created a far greater degree of chaos in family life
than any type of sexualized activity. Violent temper tantrums, physical
abuse, self-mutilation, alcohol and drug abuse, and suicidal behaviour
were distressing not only for adults in the family, but also for other
children.

Perhaps the most serious issue families had to face was when other children in the family began to copy the abused child's anti-social or disruptive behaviour. This did not seem to be a problem for natural children; but other foster and adoptive children who had been deprived themselves were exceptionally vulnerable. Violent temper tantrums, scraping wrists with razor blades, trying to carve names on arms and legs, and running away were just a few examples of problematical behaviour which were copied.

Positive outcomes of such placements for other children in the family were not easy to find. The toll on family life of re-parenting a sexually abused child extended beyond the adults in the family and affected the other children also. It was often a case of other children surviving despite the placement, because of their own inner resources, rather than thriving or finding fulfilment through the experience of having an abused child in their household. There were one or two instances where the relationship with another child in the family was the most positive aspect of the placement, but these situations were the exception rather than the rule. Some parents felt sure that the openness on sexual issues which the placement had introduced could only be beneficial for their other children as they grew towards adolescence and adulthood. In a study of this nature, such predictions about the longer term effects on other children are, of course, impossible to estimate. What the study does convey is that in the immediate situation, there were not many positive features for the other children.

KEY FACTORS IN RELATION TO OTHER CHILDREN IN THE FAMILY

Social Workers

Talk with foster and adoptive parents about the sex education which they have provided for their own children. This may be a useful indicator about how comfortable or uncomfortable families feel about addressing sexual issues.

Foster and Adoptive Families

The importance of preparing other children in the family for
a) sexual overtures from the abused child;
b) disruptive and anti-social behaviour;
c) inevitable loss of parental attention.

Encourage all families to talk with their own children at the outset of the placement about:
a) sexualized behaviour which the child may exhibit;
b) disruptive behaviour which the child may exhibit;
c) how excessive demands from the abused chid are likely to create change for everyone in the family.

Help families to reflect on practical ways of responding to the demands of the abused child while simultaneously meeting the needs of their own children.

Arrange meetings with other experienced families to encourage realism.

Recommend books on sex education to help families.

The value of educating abused children and other children in the family **together** about sex and relationships. This prevents the abused child from feeling different to the others.

High expectations about the degree of companionship which an abused child may be able to offer other children in the family may be unrealistic – and liable to lead to disappointment.

Prepare for the likelihood of having to tackle sexualized behaviour in sibling placements. Changing this type of behaviour is likely to be difficult because it has often been learned over a protracted period.

9 Handling the reactions of people outside the family

Handling reactions inside the family was just one area of difficulty for foster and adoptive families. There was, of course, a wider range of people affected by the placement, including the extended family, neighbours, friends and indeed anyone with whom the abused child came into contact. Pacifying feelings, clarifying misunderstandings and tactfully educating everyone concerned was time-consuming and often exasperating. The fact that the abused child looked normal created an immediate barrier to understanding. People found it difficult to comprehend the child's inner problems because there was no immediate evidence of physical or mental disability.

SEXUAL BEHAVIOUR TOWARDS ADULTS OUTSIDE THE FAMILY

Embarrassing moments occurred when children used inappropriate sexual language or behaved sexually in the company of relatives, neighbours, friends or even total strangers. Peter (12) was placed with a single parent. When the front door bell would ring, he would rush to answer it and eagerly enquire: 'Have you come to have sex with my mum?' Barry (13) was obsessed with his developing anatomy. He would stride up to a total stranger and announce: 'I have hair growing on my cock. Do you want to see it?' Samantha (10) was convinced that everyone would be interested in her sexual history. As soon as she succeeded in getting the attention of an adult, she would ask unashamedly: 'Will I tell them about Phil's willy?'

Children might cause a sensation in social settings by boasting of their sexual achievements and using words and phrases which created ripples of shock throughout the entire company. Teenage girls chose their moment for appearing in the living room in their most transparent nightdress.

Sometimes it was sexualized actions which presented the greatest problem. Some families had learned the art of preventing relatives or friends from sitting on their living room settee because they knew that the child would inevitably move into the adjacent seat and that trouble would ensue: 'She just couldn't sit beside a man without touching and tapping him and wanting to be touched.' The age of the adult concerned seemed to be immaterial: 'Even if he was a 75-year-old-man with no teeth and a walking stick, he would still be approached.'

Some people coped with these situations in a straightforward manner. Simple tactics were often most effective: 'Rachel (6) was very forward and suggestive with my neighbour's husband. She was like a 15-year-old flirting, kissing and cuddling and trying to get on his lap. He handled it well. He would just stand up or pick up one of his own children.' Others, however, found these incidents extremely difficult to manage: 'Audrey was obsessed with tits. Everyone had to have tits. Even although I had prepared my sister – when Audrey touched her she nearly died.'

The family were sometimes caught off-guard. A prying neighbour would ask blunt questions about the abused child's background and wait eagerly for a reply. When Court cases made headlines in the local press, some families struggled to find appropriate answers to inopportune questions from local people.

Occasionally, a relative or friend's manner of communication with the child merely reinforced sexualized behaviour. Education was essential to enable them to adopt a more helpful approach: 'One friend took a flirty approach. She used to say "Mark, you're looking lovely!" He used to grovel to her in an adult manner. She was very cuddly to him and he used to misinterpret. I had to talk to her. She took on board what I was saying.'

It was harder to explain to others who were completely naive:

She was so confused. She didn't know who was doing what. We thought that she might make an allegation against the vicar. If I said to the Sunday School teacher 'You're at risk', they would think that I was daft. She went to a Youth Club run by a Catholic Order of monks. Her behaviour was so sexual. They couldn't handle it. They had no idea.

Some relatives and friends found the entire experience so disconcerting that they made a hasty retreat from the family.

Criticisms were frequently levelled at families because of the way in which they were parenting the abused child. People described some families' level of supervision of children and adolescents as 'completely over the top'. Comments like 'She's a lovely girl' or 'Isn't he affectionate?' made some foster and adoptive families cringe. There were stresses associated with explaining and re-explaining a method of parenting which could be perceived as extreme by people with no knowledge of sexually abused children.

Tradesmen visiting the home presented a special problem. In some instances, they completed their work in record time in order to make a speedy escape:

> We have never had tradesmen in and out of our house so quickly. She latches on to any male. People tend to be so naive. A ten-year-old saying to a joiner 'Gosh, you've got a lovely bum' – people think it can't be true – and they look at us as much as to say 'What kind of family is this?'

In another case, a six-year-old girl used to appear in the nude at the bedroom window in full view of the workmen who were building an extension to the house. It was not only girls who adopted this approach: 'This guy came to repair our central heating system. Martyn (6) crouched down and started stroking down his body and saying "I love you". You should have seen his face.'

The difficulties associated with these situations were compounded and overshadowed by the issue of confidentiality which left some families confused and bewildered. Staff in some Social Services Departments had emphasized the vital importance of keeping the sexual abuse aspect of the case confidential. Conflicts occurred. Families did not want to breach departmental policy, but they found themselves forced to do so. People outside the family who became involved in sexualized incidents required some kind of explanation. Concealing the fact of sexual abuse often exposed the child to an unnecessary degree of misunderstanding and insensitivity.

SEXUAL BEHAVIOUR TOWARDS CHILDREN AND TEENAGERS OUTSIDE THE FAMILY

Foster and adoptive families reminisced about the embarrassment associated with the abused child becoming involved in a sexual incident with another child outside the family. These incidents were much more easily handled when they happened inside the immediate family circle. When they occurred outside, there were additional stresses associated with placating the feelings of everyone involved. It was even more traumatic when these episodes produced the first hint of sexual abuse:

> Our seven-year-old foster boy went to tea with a friend. The first we knew about sexual abuse was when we discovered that he had been found in bed in the nude with our friend's six-year-old girl, trying to perform the sexual act. To him that was normal. I was very shocked and stunned. My first reaction was 'He will have to be moved'.

Allowing a child to play in the neighbourhood could sometimes present tensions. Abused children often had difficulty in making friends. It was not easy to encourage them to take the initiative with other children and at the same time ensure that these relationships were retained within appropriate limits: 'His play is much too involved. His way of playing is sexual. He gives the children piggy-backs and rubs them up. He jumps on the children and presses himself against them. I have to call him indoors when I see it happening.'

These difficulties did not just happen in the neighbourhood. At school there were problems with sexual language; sexual drawings affecting other classmates; girls and boys exposing themselves; children being bullied when they refused to comply with requests for kissing and fondling. Sometimes abused children needed one-to-one supervision in changing rooms, at a swimming class or during lunch break.

All the children who had been subjected to sexual abuse were not necessarily sexually precocious. Some were exactly the opposite, and therefore especially vulnerable within the school setting: 'There was trouble at school with a child from a broken home who was in the same class as Susan. She was doing sexual things in the classroom. Susan would sob for hours.'

Some children had no idea about boundaries in relationships with other children. Talking indiscriminately to their schoolmates about their story of abuse often had disastrous consequences:

> Gill would tell the children in the playground and gather a crowd around her. Then she would come home from school and say that the other children were calling her 'prostitute'. The children were not sympathetic. Her idea was that if she told at school, everyone would treat her as 'different' and 'special'.

As classmates related these stories at home, some parents panicked. They instructed their child to sever all connections with the abused child immediately. In this way, some special friendships were broken, leaving abused children hurt and confused and foster and adoptive families shocked at the lack of sensitivity displayed.

Teenagers had additional problems knowing how to handle their developing sexuality. Some were giving out clear sexual messages without meaning to do so:

> All her attitudes to males were 'Come and get me', and yet the last thing she wanted was a sexual relationship . . . A boy asked her if she would sleep with him. She doesn't want to. She hasn't got sexuality worked out. She's very muddled. It's difficult to steer her into a normal view of sex. She is nowhere near taking responsibility for herself. She's strong, she's weak and she's muddled.

Other teenagers retreated from any form of physical contact with the opposite sex: 'She wants no sexuality. She's terrified of sex and very nervous when she gets a boyfriend. She never keeps a relationship long.' Occasionally, teenagers alleged that one of their peers had sexually abused them. Generally, families adopted a protective approach towards the accused by handling the situation themselves rather than reporting it to their Social Services Department:

> She accused a 14-year-old boy of beating her arm with his penis. His mother said 'Do you think that we should call the Police?' I said 'No'. You cannot blame a 14-year-old for triggering behaviour. Jane was so confused. She just did not know who was doing what. We kept the incident to ourselves.

In at least two placements which disrupted, teenagers were know to have turned to a lifestyle of prostitution.

KEY ISSUES

Social Workers

Consider including key people in foster/adoptive families' social network in training on child sexual abuse.

Foster and Adoptive Families

1   Discuss the following issues with social worker:

a) Who should know about the child's history of sexual abuse?

b) How much should they know?

c) What type of cover story

should be used with people who may ask direct questions, but who do not really require to know?

2   (a), (b) and (c) may also need to be worked on with abused children who talk indiscriminately to everyone about their history of sexual abuse.

10 Access to birth families

All adoptive and foster families tackle a unique type of parenting which can never totally exclude the child's original family. Even if there is no direct contact between children and their birth families, substitute families face the complex task of helping children come to terms with their past. Abused children require help to understand the positive and negative events in their life history and the factors which necessitated their reception into care.

ADOPTION PLACEMENTS

None of the children in adoption placements continued to see their birth parents. One teenager did write annually to her birth mother at Christmas. Four children occasionally visited their siblings who were either fostered or adopted by other families. Another child retained contact with an aunt, uncle and grandparents. Although these relationships were often initiated with enthusiasm, there was a tendency for them to dwindle as children became more fully integrated into their adoptive family.

Occasionally, sexualized behaviour between siblings became a problem when access occurred. In one adoption placement, where a brother sometimes stayed overnight with the adoptive family, sexual touching between the boys immediately evidenced itself. In another placement, where an eight-year-old girl yearned to see her brother, but was being denied access, she had no hesitation in acknowledging that she wanted to renew a sexual relationship with him.

Four adoptive families had met the birth parents on one occasion. Another two were planning to do so in the future. This meeting was usually organized by the social worker, believing that it would be for the mutual benefit of everyone concerned. Adopters remembered how they had approached the meeting with apprehension. Looking back, they all felt exceptionally positive about the experience, and were glad that they had summoned enough courage to proceed with it. When one of the birth parents was the abuser, face to face contact had the effect of transforming adopters' negative attitudes. Perpetrators who had been visualized as 'ogres' and 'monsters' became real people who were more likely to be perceived as 'pathetic' and 'inadequate'. Following these meetings, adopters were convinced that there would be immediate and longer-term benefits for their adopted child as they now felt able to talk about the abuser in a more comfortable and informed manner.

There were special problems for adopters who wanted to make contact with birth parents when an allegation of sexual abuse had been substantiated against previous substitute carers. Naturally, they worried about how they could begin to build trust when this had been so completely undermined by other foster carers. Two adoptive families were worrying about these issues at the time of being interviewed for this study.

FOSTERING PLACEMENTS

Fostering placements presented a far greater degree of complexity in relation to access. In 38 out of 57 placements (67 per cent), foster children continued to retain some contact with their birth parents. Sometimes, children returned home for access visits. More commonly, birth parents visited the foster home or met their child in a more neutral setting such as the social services office.

It was often very difficult for children to make attachments within their foster family while simultaneously coping with family loyalties. Some foster families had completely unrealistic expectations about this. Sexual abuse had so many negative connotations for themselves that they assumed that any child who had been sexually abused by a birth parent would automatically reject that parent and make very quick and meaningful attachments within the foster family. Children rarely demonstrated one clear emotion towards the perpetrator, however, and conflicting loyalties and confusion were more characteristic. Consequently, some foster families found this type of parenting much less fulfilling than they had originally anticipated.

I was green to start with. They still love their families. That was hard to understand at the beginning. I really wanted to foster the girls. I wanted to mother them, but they found it difficult to confide or talk. We're just plastic parents. Their own parents are the real ones.

Some foster carers felt that they were expected to carry too much responsibility for access visits. This was particularly true when access occurred in the foster home, involving the alleged perpetrator. Some foster carers felt responsible not only for supervising the relationship between the perpretrator and the foster child, but also for monitoring all the movements of the other children in the family to ensure that they were not placed at risk too. In several cases, a birth parent made violent threats or alleged that the foster carers were guilty of sexual misconduct towards the child. One foster carer who had just completed an affidavit for court talked about the burden of having to face a verbally abusive father whom she had implicated in her legal document. Again and again, access which began in the foster home had to be transferred elsewhere because the level of stress on the foster family became intolerable.

When access visits took place in a neutral setting, other problems could occur. Several families complained because social workers failed to keep them informed about the interaction which occurred. This excluded foster carers from a vital part of the child's life and left them totally dependent on guesswork or a subjective interpretation of the child's verbal or non-verbal communication after the visit.

Even when access to a birth parent was disallowed, there was no guarantee that a chance meeting might not occur. This happened in several instances and was one of the disadvantages of making placements in the immediate locality of the child's own home. An unexpected encounter with her father while shopping caused so much distress for one child that it culminated in her first disclosure.

Gifts had a special significance for a number of abused children. Some had received gifts as part of the ritual associated with sexual abuse. When gifts were produced by the perpetrator or by anyone else during access visits, this could trigger a series of memories for the child. Sometimes gifts had the effect of reinstigating patterns of sexualized behaviour which seemed previously to have disappeared. Even when there was no direct access, monetary gifts could arrive by post from relatives. Some children were too angry with their birth family to accept these favours. Several children opted to return the money.

Some children's anger was directed not so much towards the perpetrator as towards the parent who had failed to protect them from sexual abuse. One teenager who had been sexually abused by her father felt so angry with her mother that she wrote her a lengthy and vicious letter. Nothing would stop her in her resolve to accost her mother personally with this letter. In an outburst of anger, her mother threw the letter at her, declaring that she never wanted to see her again. The foster family spent the ensuing weeks and months helping this girl cope with the devastation associated with this experience.

Handling the aftermath of access visits was one of the very difficult tasks which foster carers had to tackle. Sometimes it was a case of responding to the child's shattered hopes when a parent who had promised to visit failed to appear. Problem behaviour usually reached a peak before and after access visits. There are clear instances in this study of children's anger towards their birth family being completely transferred on to the foster carer. In extreme instances, foster carers were attacked physically immediately following an access visit, and left with serious lacerations and bruising.

Telephone access between children and their birth family was another difficult area. It is easy to forget how much stress can be engendered by this type of contact. Some of the most distressing outbursts took place immediately after children replaced the telephone receiver: 'We had the most terrible trouble after phone calls. He had a terrific amount of anger inside. He suffered from petit mal and he would blank out. He was totally out of control, stamping on the dog, punching my wife up and tearing the wallpaper off the wall.'

Another teenager who made several suicide attempts always took this action immediately following a telephone conversation with her father who had sexually abused her.

KEY ISSUES RELATED TO ACCESS

Social Workers

Access Visits:
Where should access occur? In the foster home or elsewhere?

If access occurs outside the foster home, it is essential that social workers make time to share information with

Foster and Adoptive Families

Children's sense of loyalty towards their birth family will not automatically be destroyed as a result of sexual abuse. These loyalties are likely to continue to affect the child's ability to create bonds with the substitute family.

foster carers about the interaction that occurs.

Support during access visits: Who should be present? Is it too threatening for the foster family to manage this alone?

Telephone Access:
The difficulties associated with telephone access can easily be disregarded despite the inherent stresses associated with it and its tendency to trigger a crisis.

Some children's anger may focus primarily on the parent who failed to protect them from sexual abuse, rather than on the perpetrator.

Children's angry feelings towards a birth parent may become displaced. Revengeful physical onslaughts, intended for the birth parent, may be directed at the immediate carer.

Gifts: it is important to be aware that there may be complications for abused children associated with receiving gifts when these have been part of the child's original experience of abuse.

The positive value for adopters of meeting the birth parents should not be overlooked. This has particular significance when sexual abuse has occurred within the birth family. Adopters in this study who met the perpetrator felt that this helped them to feel more comfortable about explaining background facts to their child.

11   *The trauma of allegations*

Any allegation of misconduct made against a substitute family is inherently stressful. When the accusation concerns sexual abuse and is made by a child, feelings are heightened. After years of stifling children's attempts to talk about personal experiences of sexual abuse, the emphasis today centres on the need for professionals to believe the child. This has immediate repercussions for any substitute family caring for a sexually abused child.

This chapter is principally concerned with the impact on the substitute family when such an allegation occurs. Of course, it has to be recognized that this is only one perspective on this very emotive subject. There is also much that needs to be learned about the abused child who makes the allegation and about the trauma for professionals who are directly involved at this point of crisis. As this study only included interviews with the substitute family and not with the other people immediately involved, this chapter focuses exclusively on the experiences of foster and adoptive families.

Three children in this study made allegations of sexual abuse against a member of their foster or adoptive family. In one instance, an 11-year-old boy accused his adoptive mother. The other two were made against foster fathers by teenage girls. These accusations had a powerful impact, producing immediate action by professionals and sometimes overturning years of work within the course of a few hours. This action not only threatened the stability of the placement, but also cast a shadow over the accused family's future role in fostering or adoption. Allegations brought experienced foster families in this study to the most critical point they had ever reached in their fostering career. Years of experience and expertise counted for nothing if their innocence could not be established.

Interviews with families who had experienced allegations of sexual abuse highlighted so many key issues that it seemed worthwhile approaching several social services departments with a specific request to increase the sample of families who could talk from experience about allegations. Obtaining permission to interview families in this category proved to be very difficult. Five statutory departments were contacted; all declined permission. The reasons given for these negative responses were interesting in themselves. More than one official from a social services department stated that foster families within their area, who had had to contend with allegations, felt angry and disillusioned with their department because of the poor quality of service they had been offered. Under these circumstances, they considered it inappropriate to nominate such families for this study. Such comments are themselves indicators of how essential it is for this aspect of fostering and adoption work to be studied more fully so that meaningful guidelines and effective support services can be established.

'No one forewarned us about allegations' was the angry retort of one foster family. This family was caught completely unawares when their foster teenager turned their tranquil lifestyle upside down by asserting that a sexual incident had occurred between herself and her foster father. This absence of preparation was a common feature. Some families seemed startled by the question posed on the interview schedule: 'Were you ever concerned that this child might make an allegation against you?' The family who replied 'What difference would it make if she did make an allegation? We had a blind faith in ourselves and in our children' had clearly never grasped the powerful nature of an allegation, regardless of their guilt or innocence. Responses indicated that in as many as 23 out of 66 families (35 per cent), the idea that they might be accused of sexual malpractice had not even crossed their minds. An absence of basic information resulted in some families engaging in a reckless type of parenting which failed to take cognisance of the child's sexual history. For example, some foster fathers never considered the risk element associated with undertaking childsitting single handed. In one case where the foster father was on night shift, he made a regular practice of taking his nine-year-old foster daughter into bed with him in the mornings after his wife had left for work. In another case, a 17-year-old adoptee, who had a very deprived background, was frequently left to childsit for two young girls, who both had a history of sexual abuse. In this way, families placed themselves in excessively vulnerable situations. The fact that allegations did not occur in a much larger proportion of cases could only be attributed to good luck rather than to careful and well-informed parenting.

When an allegation occurred, one of the greatest difficulties confronting families was a basic lack of information about what was happening at all stages. Sometimes, proceedings were already under way before the accused family was made aware of the exact nature of the allegation. Vivid descriptions were given by families of feelings of 'powerlessness', 'ostracism' and 'being branded as criminals'. Eleven-year-old Christopher's adoptive parents still feel hurt by the manner in which they were treated by officialdom:

> Christopher ran away and landed at a police station. We were called to pick him up. We arrived at the police station on the simple pretext of collecting our son. I sat outside in the car while my husband went inside. He was shown into an interview room. The first he knew that something was wrong was when the key was turned in the lock. The room was only eight feet square. Three quarters of an hour later, he was still there. We could only assume that there had been an allegation. We had no idea who the allegation was against, and whether it was of physical or sexual abuse. No one told us . . . I saw Christopher being taken away in a police car. I could only assume that he was being taken to hospital for a medical examination.

Other features of such allegations which emerged in different family situations are worth noting:

a) An incident occurred immediately prior to the allegation which left the abused child distressed and aggrieved.
b) The experience of allegations was totally devastating for the entire family. The healing process was slow and could stretch over years.
c) Allegations frequently produced a panic response from professionals with an absence of careful planning for the child. (One child-centred family would have preferred the accused family member to have been removed to allow the enquiry to proceed, rather than destroying all their years of work by an abrupt removal of the child.)
d) The process of investigation was experienced as both intrusive and stressful.
e) Families felt demoted from their status as 'colleague' and were often excluded from crucial meetings.
f) There was no independent forum or independent individual to whom the family could express strong emotions, or with whom they could discuss the effects of events on their family.
g) The serious impact on other children in the family was largely ignored. No support network existed for them.
h) Even when the allegation was disproved, the family were not given

any form of written statement from the agency dealing with the complaint. They felt stigmatised for life.

All these features appear in the Brown family record of their experiences. After 12 years' fostering experience, their world fell apart as they found themselves accused of sexual abuse by Cheryl, a 12-year-old girl whom they had been fostering for almost two years. This is how the foster mother recorded there story:

> There were warning signs. Cheryl made an allegation against a 14-year-old boy who was a friend's son. You couldn't blame a 14-year-old for triggering behaviour. She was so confused. She did not know who was doing what. We kept this incident to ourselves and then told social services later. We were worried about the vicar. We thought that she might accuse him . . .
>
> Cheryl was upset about a dancing competition. She had not practised for it and ended up being last in the competition . . . During the same weekend, my husband needed to go to the video shop to return a video. He took Cheryl and our five-year-old boy, Martin. He parked outside the video shop and told Martin to run into the shop and straight out again, because of the way he was parked. Martin was only in there a few seconds . . .
>
> The next day, Cheryl went to school as usual. During the day, she confided in a teacher. She said that she had fallen on the bed with my husband the previous day. Although nothing had happened, she had felt uncomfortable. She went on to say that while Martin was in the video shop, my husband had said to her:
>
> 'I have a loving wife and a lovely family and a 12-year-old foster daughter whom I want to screw.'
>
> We knew nothing about the allegation. the Headteacher had been unable to report the incident to social services on that day. Cheryl returned home as usual.
>
> That evening, Cheryl seemed very low. She was extra helpful. She did all her homework and then wanted to do the dishes. The next morning she got up very early. She kissed us both 'Goodbye' and left for school. That was two years ago now, and that was the last we saw of Cheryl. She was moved that day, and we were investigated.
>
> They took her to an Assessment Unit. They could not hold her. She's on the run. If the police pick her up she will go to a secure unit. They should not have moved her. (They could have moved my husband for a few days until everything got sorted out.) Within 48 hours, it was clear that the allegation was false. She was so muddled.

She had changed her story so many times. Within two days, she could have been back here. She would have gone through the misery with us – the anger and the disappointment – but we could all have worked on it together, and within a week been functioning together as a family.

We all suffered. A few weeks ago, I saw a headline in the newspaper 'Abuse arrest drove fosterer to suicide'. That summed up the pain we experienced. It was not so much that I wanted to die. I remember feeling that I wanted annihilation. It was the most dreadful thing that we ever lived through. In some ways, it was worse for my husband. At least I would cry. When things got bad for him, he put up barriers. I even asked him 'Did you say it?' Suddenly I was thrown into confusion. 'Do I know my husband?' I thought, 'Can he possibly be a child abuser?' I was not sure any more.

My husband was not up to Cheryl. He didn't get the measure of her. She caused rifts between us. He doesn't have an inbuilt second nature. That is what you need with a child like Cheryl. Did Cheryl want a relationship with my husband like the one she had with her abuser? Well, we will never know.

All the children were affected. There was a lot of anger around Cheryl. They didn't like her. She didn't like them. She stole. She smeared faeces in their toys and clothes. It was a grotty two year experience for them. I still feel (two years later) that there's a lot of unresolved anger.

One social worker said that, because Cheryl made the allegation, that we had failed to protect her. By my husband being on his own with her, he had given her false messages. Social workers do not have the experience. They said that there would be no secrets from us. They had all the secrets in the world. The whole experience left us with so little – so little privacy. Everything in our lives was exposed. It leaves you raw. It leaves you naked. You have to forage for support.

We needed someone to let us talk. Apart from my foster friend, there was no one to sound off to. Cheryl leaving us was like living through the death of a child. It has taken two years, and we are still mourning. We needed someone to take us through the bereavement, but there was nothing from social services. Individual social workers who knew the way that we had worked in the past tried to support us, but they just did not have the power to influence the decisions that were made.

Now Cheryl is in a worse state than she has ever been in. The last we heard of her she was into prostitution and drugs and there's no chance of stopping the downward spiral. I have no doubt in my mind which option would have been better for her.

Cheryl's foster family were typical of others in that they had an intuitive hunch that an allegation was imminent. Attempts to alert professionals to this fact were often disregarded. The following comment was made by another foster family who felt that their pleas for help produced a stony professional silence: 'For weeks I had been saying "Do something. If you don't help me, something dreadful is going to happen".'

As soon as an allegation occurred, this silence was immediately broken and exchanged for frenzied professional activity. Families felt aggrieved that their warnings had been ignored. Even if the allegation was inevitable, they felt strongly that their reputation could have been safeguarded if the risk factor to them had been carefully monitored.

It was noticeable that the sexual allegation which caused such havoc in foster and adoptive homes was often relatively minor, compared to the sexual trauma which the child had experienced prior to 'reception into care'. The following are a few examples: 'He put his hand on the top of the eiderdown on my bed'; 'He said that he wanted to screw me'; 'He pushed me on the bed, but nothing happened'.

Disruptions frequently occurred at the point of allegation. As the Brown's story illustrates, such a major action could have been averted in their case if they had been fully consulted. Of course, all the families were not quite as magnanimous as the Browns. Another family were too angry to re-admit the child into their family circle and would certainly not have countenanced the idea of excluding the accused adult from their family on a temporary basis. Sometimes it was the other children's sense of loyalty to the accused family member which made them adamant that the abused child would never again cross their threshold.

All the families in this study were able to continue with their adoption and fostering work after the allegation had been investigated. One family was the first in their social services department to face this trauma. Their social worker resigned as a mark of protest against her department's inadequate system of support. Although everyone suffered in this particular case, it was instrumental in alerting professionals to the need for new guidelines and procedures associated with allegations. Families who were regular members of a fostering group often awakened a new sensitivity and awareness among other foster families on this crucial topic.

In order to obtain a balanced perspective on this subject, it is important to refer back to chapter 1 which outlines who the perpetrator or alleged perpetrator was in each case in this study. It is worth remembering that eight children had originally been sexually abused within a foster or adoptive family. Even when social workers may consider that they have undertaken the most thorough assessment and preparation of a substitute family, it is essential for them to recognize the possibility that sexual abuse could still occur within this foster or adoptive family.

On the other hand, the allegations of sexual abuse against foster carers discussed in this chapter were not substantiated. Following investigations, it became clear that they were untrue. The precise reasons the allegations were made are not clear. Did they occur as a result of the abused child's confusion? Were they the response of an angry child immediately following an experience of personal disappointment? Was it the child's way of saying 'I want out of this family?' Such detailed information is beyond the scope of this study.

Currently there is considerable emphasis on the importance of professionals listening to the child and believing the child's story of abuse. This emphasis has major implications for substitute families. It is likely to make them feel exceptionally vulnerable. It is grossly unfair to expect substitute families to take on a sexually abused child without explaining to them how crucial the abused child's words will be if any allegation does occur. Every foster and adoptive family needs to think about how to organize their daily living so that the abused child derives maximum benefit while at the same time safeguarding themselves from becoming easy targets of an allegation of sexual abuse.

The following recommendations derive from the experiences of families who lived through the trauma of allegations:

a) Every local authority and voluntary agency needs to devise clear guidelines for handling allegations.
b) The importance of alerting every foster and adoptive family to the potential risk of allegations of sexual abuse being made against them.
c) Familiarize every substitute family with departmental guidelines so that they know what to expect should an allegation occur.
d) Provide every substitute family with the opportunity to consider changes which may be essential in their lifestyle to protect all family members against allegations. Repeat this exercise in a specific way whenever a new placement occurs, taking into consideration the unique factors in each child's history.
e) Ensure that the following issues are clarified at the outset of the placement:
   – Who will offer support should an allegation occur?
   – What type of support will be available (including support for other children in the family)?
   – For what length of time will support be available?

Foster and adoptive families stressed that it was difficult for social workers immediately associated with the placement to detach themselves from departmental loyalties and to provide an effective 'listening ear' and objective advice and consultation. They recommend that an independent counsellor with professional knowledge and competence in sexual abuse work be appointed to provide support.

f) Important principles in relation to allegations:

Preplanning – It is important to listen to substitute families' warnings about allegations and to examine ways of preventing allegations becoming a reality.

Communication – Open communication with families is vital. 'Secret' meetings merely exacerbate feelings of ostracism. Lack of knowledge about what is happening increases anxiety and resentment.

Planning for the child – Explore options for the abused child. Even an angry substitute family may prefer the accused to be removed temporarily from the family rather than upsetting years of hard work by the sudden removal of the abused child.

Termination of contact – When a placement does have to be terminated, it is important to remember basic childcare principles. The need for all parties to say 'Goodbye' is not any less important when a placement disrupts because of an allegation than for any other reason.

KEY ISSUES: CHANGES IN LIFESTYLE TO PROTECT AGAINST ALLEGATIONS

a) Privacy

Lock on bathroom door.
Everyone wearing a dressing gown.
No one appearing scantily clad.

b) Bedroom/bathroom rules

Children not allowed into adults' bedroom.
Children not going into each others' bedrooms.
Separate bedrooms for sibling placements.
Not allowing abused child into adults' bed.

Foster or adoptive father not putting girls to bed or bathing girls.
Adults not having private discussions with abused child in bedroom.

c) Physical contact

Careful about physical contact with abused child and how any expression of affection in the family may be interpreted by a child with a sexual history.
Being conscious of how you allow an abused child to snuggle up to you.
Restricting the time that an abused child sits on the adult's knee when child's behaviour is sexual.
Teaching older child to sit side by side with an adult in an affectionate way rather than on adult's lap.

d) Childsitting

Never leaving any male in house on his own with an abused girl.
Childsitting in pairs.
Informing childsitters about history of sexual abuse.
Turning down friends who offer to childsit who are unwilling to acknowledge the risks involved.
Using other experienced foster carers or adopters who already have experience of sexual abuse.

e) Recording events

Keeping a regular daily diary which can be used to verify what actually occurred.
Informing social worker of any incident which made you feel uncomfortable or anxious.

12 *The vital importance of training*

Figure 9 illustrates that exceptionally few families had attended any type of training course in the issue of child sexual abuse before facing the challenge of parenting a sexually abused child. These figures appear more significant against a background of families' own conviction that an absence of training seriously impeded their potential to respond to the needs of abused children. The majority of families were very enthusiastic about participating in training if such opportunities had been made available to them.

Although some families had an amazing ability to respond intuitively to children, it was risky to depend on such a flimsy foundation. Even those who had gained an excellent reputation because of their child-centred work admitted that they were often responding to situations on a trial and error basis and consequently carrying a high level of stress. The following disadvantages were evident when families ventured into this work without training.

Figure 9 Number of adoptive and foster families who had access to training in child sexual abuse

	Access prior to placement	Access during or after placement	No access at any time
Number of Families	5	24	37
	8%	36%	56%

Total number of families: 66

a) Parenting was being undertaken in an unconfident manner.
b) Opportunities for enabling children to talk about their personal experiences of abuse were sometimes missed because the importance of disclosure had not been grasped.
c) Inappropriate patterns of sexualized behaviour were sometimes being reinforced as a result of lack of knowledge.
d) One factor in some placements which disrupted was lack of preparation for the intrusive and disruptive influence which an abused child could have on their family life.
e) Some families failed to protect themselves against the threat of allegations because they were unaware of their vulnerability.

Even families who did have the opportunity to attend training sometimes only spent a couple of hours on the subject of sexual abuse. Some talked about attending a seminar or conference on child abuse with sexual abuse being only a very small component of the total programme. Others participated in a general preparation course in adoption with scant reference being made to sexually abused children. The more detailed and comprehensive courses tended to be a recent phenomenon. In fact, some families were undertaking their first training programme at the same time as this study occurred. Many felt that the experience had 'arrived too late' to be of maximum benefit to them. There was no evidence that the 37 families who had never had access to training were likely to receive this in the near future.

In some authorities, training in sexual abuse was offered exclusively to professionals. This evoked angry and resentful feelings from some families:

> Social workers get bloody good money for going on courses. You ring up. They're never there. Where are they? On a course on sexual abuse. When I ask for advice, they have no answers. They just say 'What do you think?' They're the ones who go on all the bloody courses. They should be able to advise. If I had got the chance to go, I would have known myself.

At least five foster families paid their own fees to attend relevant training courses after their local authority refused to sponsor them. Three families had been prepared to spend in excess of £350 from their personal savings in order to attend a residential training course.

Whether training occurred during the pre-placement or post-placement period, the benefits were many. Every family could find something positive to say about the experience. Acquiring basic factual knowledge about sexual abuse reduced anxiety and inspired confidence. One family reminisced about the helpful aspects for them: 'It makes you look at your own sexuality. It makes you rethink your parenting of your own children. The fact that we had been on a training course helped us to keep calm at the time of disclosure.'

Others enthused about discovering new and stimulating ideas; recognizing that their particular child's problems were not unique; and returning home with a more balanced perspective on the problems confronting them.

Attending training was often the trigger which enabled individuals who had suffered sexual abuse themselves to confront the trauma associated with this. Sometimes video material had such an overwhelming impact on victims of abuse that they felt compelled to disclose 'secrets' in their own lives. It was vital that families had the opportunity to discuss their own abuse to prevent these powerful emotions from affecting the placement. One foster carer described how role play was instrumental in bringing her into touch with the pain of her abuse which she had suppressed for years: 'It started to unravel itself through training. Taking on the role of the abuser brought it back. I realized when I was acting out the role of the perpetrator that I wanted someone to step in and stop me. That was a tremendous relief.'

There were also some criticisms made in relation to training:

a) There was not enough training available (even those who had attended in-depth training would have welcomed additional opportunities to learn more on this crucial theme).

b) Training often failed to address issues connected with everyday living:

It needs to be more down to earth – to deal with the 'nitty gritty'. What do you do if a child takes his willy out on a bus? What if he comes into the bathroom and wants to 'stroke' you? What if you find the abused child in bed with your own child? It's spotting it and living it. That is what you need to know about.

c) Occasionally, training programmes lacked a balanced approach. Focusing on too many negative factors could be frightening. Some families felt that they would have withdrawn from fostering or adoption following training, if they had not been able to use their own experience and direct knowledge about abused children as a ballast:

It was too shocking. It was over the top. They played on your emotions. They gave the impression 'It's terrible. It's horrible'. They showed an American film of three adults who had been abused and who had had no help. People were crying their eyes out. It was too much about feelings towards the abuser rather than about how to help the child . . . They need to tell you that there are degrees of abuse . . . It needs to be put into context.

The overall impression conveyed through the study was that it was completely unrealistic and even foolhardy for professionals to expect families to undertake this task without access to the basic facts about sexual abuse. There were also many advantages associated with opportunities for training in the post-placement period, allowing families to consolidate and extend their knowledge and also to reflect further on their practice.

KEY ISSUES: INFORMATION WHICH FAMILIES CONSIDERED SHOULD BE INCLUDED IN TRAINING

Basic information

a) Signs and symptoms of sexual abuse.
b) Behavioural patterns.
c) Insights into how the sexually abused child feels.
d) Normal sexual development and how it is affected by sexual abuse.
e) Sex offenders: insights into their problems.
f) The disruptive effect on family life of parenting sexually abused children.
g) The effect on marriages.
h) Long term effects of sexual abuse.
i) Sex education with an abused child.
j) Information about victims of abuse who have survived

Handling the difficulties

a) Handling disclosure:
   (i) 'listening' to behaviour;
   (ii) helping the 'closed' child to open up;
   (iii) how to approach the subject.
b) Helping children to grasp that sexual abuse is not their fault.
c) Ongoing disclosure work.
d) Handling inappropriate sexual behaviour.
e) Helping children who have been sexually active to survive without sex.
f) Strategies for preventing children from driving wedges in marriages.
g) Ways of protecting everyone in the family.

115

the experience.

k) Confidentiality: its meaning within the day to day context of family living.

l) Life story work (covering sexual abuse).

m) Allegations: the fact that they are liable to occur/the need to protect everyone in the family against allegations.

n) Departmental procedures:
   (i) in the event of disclosure;
   (ii) in the event of a crisis.

o) Local resources.

p) Facts about AIDS.

h) Learning to talk about sexual matters within the family.

i) Handling violence.

j) Modifying difficult behaviour.

k) Ideas on discipline.

The personal impact

a) Recognizing and handling personal reactions to sexual abuse.

b) Handling sexual feelings.

c) The impact of sexual 'touching' (for both men and women.

d) Managing own experience of sexual abuse (if appropriate).

Skills training

a) Giving evidence in Court.

b) Writing affidavits.

c) Participating in reviews and case conferences.

d) Building up contact with professionals.

e) Learning how to work as an effective member of a team.

13 *The question of therapy*

Which sexually abused children require psychotherapy? At what stage is therapy essential? These questions caused much debate and controversy. Some substitute families felt that their child urgently needed this type of specialist help and were aggrieved because their persistent pleas seemed to be ignored. Others were convinced that their work with the child was the equivalent of therapy.

Sometimes social workers endorsed the family's viewpoint. At other times they totally disagreed and tried to influence the family to accept their opinion. Hours were spent at reviews and case conferences as social workers, teachers, psychiatrists, psychologists argued on this topic. Sometimes abused children were present at meetings where these contentious issues dominated discussions about their future. Occasionally an additional professional assessment was sought as a means of clarifying this matter. In one fostering placement as many as four independent assessments were requested with no ultimate consensus of opinion.

Even when there was unanimity between the family and all the other professionals concerned about the importance of therapy, there was no guarantee that adequate resources existed to ensure that this recommendation became a reality.

The three main types of therapy used were individual, group and family therapy. Occasional references were made to children having art or drama therapy. Unfortunately, families were unable to provide specific details about these types of therapy. They usually occurred during school hours and the family were not aware of the content of these sessions.

The therapist involved could be the child's social worker, a psychologist, a psychiatrist or a trained psychotherapist.

THERAPY PRIOR TO PLACEMENT: A GAP IN THE SUBSTITUTE FAMILY'S UNDERSTANDING OF THE CHILD'S PAST

At least nine out of 80 children (11 per cent) had attended a series of individual or group therapy sessions prior to placement. This number may be an underestimate; an aura of mystery seemed to surround these sessions and foster and adoptive families were not always given information about whether a child had attended therapy prior to placement. Even when they were told this basic fact, they were rarely given any details about the content of these sessions. Consequently they commenced the placement with a significant gap in their understanding of the child's past. Some felt so disadvantaged by this situation that they made persistent pleas either to gain access to written reports or to talk directly to the original therapist. These requests were largely ignored: 'They said a flat "No". The information was confidential.'

Gaps in information about previous therapy sessions could have serious implications as the placement progressed. This is illustrated in the case of Simon (10) who had made his one and only disclosure during a therapy session several years prior to the placement. His adoptive family only received this data when the placement was on the brink of disruption. He had in fact been placed with them with the comment 'suspicion of abuse'. Later they discovered that this crucial piece of information had not only been withheld from them, it had also not been passed on to the fostering and adoption department responsible for the placement. Speaking after disruption the family commented: 'We just didn't have enough information to help him. We didn't know what we were trying to get him to face up to. Because the sexual abuse bit was not definite we never really thought of it as likely to be disruptive.'

In a final unsuccessful attempt to salvage this placement, a meeting was arranged between the original therapist, the child and the prospective adopters. During this session the child's history of sexual abuse was openly discussed by everyone. The family's comments speak volumes: 'At that meeting Simon seemed relieved to know that we knew about his abuse. If he had known that we knew it would have taken away the secrecy. That would have made a big difference to the placement.'

There was one exceptional placement where it was refreshing to catch a glimpse of therapist and adoptive family working in close harmony as the child transferred from a residential establishment into an adoption placement:

Karl (10) had been seeing a psychologist for three years on a weekly basis before he came to us. When he moved to us it changed gradually to – fortnightly – and then – monthly. After Karl had been here for about eight months the sessions stopped completely but the psychologist continued to see us. She said that we were Karl's therapists and that she was handing over to us.

The psychologist continued to phone me and offer support. We would go over together what was happening. He had never verbalized his abuse to her despite three years of work. She was amazed that he had shared the whole story with us within two to three months . . . She helped him and us enormously. Without her he would have been completely frozen.

This case stands out from others in the study. It contains several simple but very important features which were rarely evident in other cases:

a) an open sharing of information and a direct line of communication between therapist and family;
b) the therapist withdrawing from the child's life at an appropriate point but continuing to share her expertise with the family by acting in a consultative capacity;
c) a mutual acknowledgement that each had skills which could be of immense benefit to the child.

THERAPY AFTER PLACEMENT: WHO? HOW? WHAT? WHEN?

Individual therapy

Figure 10 Who provided therapy?

Psychotherapist	Psychologist	Psychiatrist	Social Worker
1	8	8	8

Total: 25

Twenty-five out of 80 children (31 per cent) received therapy on an individual basis after placement. Figure 10 illustrates which professional

119

was responsible for therapy. Were foster and adoptive families concerned about who provided this service? Several families expressed dissatisfaction when social workers provided therapy. Generally, social workers were not perceived as having adequate training or relevant skills to undertake this specialist work. There were two exceptions to this. One was a social worker with specialist experience in sexual abuse whose ability to work directly with two abused teenage boys was immediately apparent. The other was a social worker whom the family knew was working under the auspices of a consultant psychiatrist, whose expertise in child sexual abuse was well known. The family described her as 'more than just an average social worker'.

How was therapy explained to the family? Very little time seemed to be spent talking with families about the rationale behind introducing therapy at a particular stage of the placement, what it would entail and what it aimed to achieve. Even in adoption placements it was sometimes imposed without any meaningful dialogue with the family or any real interest in whether they felt positively or negatively about it. Even more crucial, there did not seem to be any attempt to monitor the ongoing impact of therapy on the placement by asking the family whether they felt that it was proving to be helpful or unhelpful for the child. Even when the family was totally excluded from the entire process they still had to handle reactions from the child before and after these sessions. Uncontrollable outbursts of temper, wrecked furniture, torn clothes, soiling, bedwetting, nightmares and suicidal tendencies were just a few examples of difficulties triggered by therapy. It was easy for families who felt excluded in this way to resent therapy because it unearthed a host of new behavioural problems which upset household routines and pushed their level of tolerance to the ultimate limit.

The most common model of therapy used throughout this study involved the therapist working in an exclusive manner with the child. All other interested parties were excluded from this relationship, including the substitute family. There were, of course, degrees of exclusion, but in many cases the therapist made no attempt to absorb any information from the substitute family about their day-to-day experiences with the child, nor were the family informed about the content of therapy sessions. In extreme cases, the family were told not to 'meddle' with the sexual abuse aspect of the child's life. Instead they should recognize this specialist area as the exclusive territory of the 'expert'. The following quotation concerns a bridge fostering placement, set up with clear boundaries and tasks for everyone concerned:

We took the kids on with a package. They were to be taken out of school once a week and seen by a therapist. We were told that we were not to deal with the sexual abuse side at all. Our task was to provide a stimulating home life. The whole sexual abuse thing was to be handed over to the therapist.

Adoption placements were handled similarly. Anthony (12) was placed with a single parent. The therapist made his position clear from the outset. He did not want to receive any information about the child's day-to-day living with his substitute family. The single parent adopter was sceptical about the effectiveness of therapy when it was happening in isolation from all the other factors which impinged on the child's life:

I have very mixed feelings about therapy. The psychotherapist has said 'I don't want to know what is going on in the family. I prefer to see the child cold'. The social worker has said that the therapist doesn't want to be influenced by outside factors. How can you work with a child and his problems in isolation from the home? It doesn't make sense to me. The child is part of its environment. How can you possibly do anything constructive with the child if you ignore the environment?

One of the most remarkable aspects of this placement was that although the therapist stated that he did not want to receive information about the child's everyday life, he still found it possible to pronounce a devastating verdict on the placement: 'In my professional opinion, this child is beyond help. He is so disintegrated. He needs 24 hour professional input. He should not be in this family. Salvage the family and put the child in an institution.'

Every therapy session was not set up in quite such an exclusive manner. There was a small number of placements where a slightly different model operated. In four placements the therapist worked on an individual basis with the child but the significant difference was that the therapist's door remained open for the family to seek consultation in relation to any issue that they found difficult to handle. In these situations the family were able to inform the therapist about any new developments with the child and simultaneously seek advice about how they should respond. At the same time, the therapist was able to incorporate new information into therapy sessions. Access to the therapist made a enormous difference to the substitute family. The key aspect seemed to be that the family felt valued and that they were at least attempting to work in partnership with the therapist.

What happened during therapy sessions? The following example concerns a fostering placement of siblings (aged eight and six). It is undoubtedly the most extreme example in the study of a therapist working in complete isolation from the substitute family, but it does portray features which were repeated in other placements in a less obvious manner. The family expressed concern about whether this method of working merely reproduced echoes of the children's original experience of abuse which so often contained phrases like 'It's a secret' or 'Don't tell anyone':

> Every week the therapist sees the children in a locked room. They have been given keys for unlocking their hearts and locking them up again. They've been given books in which they write their secrets but they are not to tell anyone except the therapist what they write in the books. The secrets issue has caused friction between the girls. At reviews, the therapist will not tell anyone what happens in these sessions. She says that it is up to her to keep confidentiality.

There was clear evidence that this way of working blocked the child's ability to communicate freely about sexual abuse with the substitute family. In one placement the adopters escorted their eight-year-old girl 80 miles to and from therapy every week. On one occasion when the adoptive father was driving home, he casually asked her 'How did you get on today?' She immediately retorted: 'I can't tell you. It's a secret between me and my therapist.'

The fact that there was a barrier of silence between the therapist and the family also created other difficulties. Some families felt that it resulted in a very unsatisfactory and fragmented approach to their child's problems. This is illustrated in the placement of a nine-year-old girl who was demonstrating very sexualized behaviour towards her adoptive father. This situation had built up over several months and had gradually resulted in the adoptive mother feeling more and more angry, embittered and extremely jealous. Where could they turn for help? The child was involved in regular therapy and so it seemed logical to turn in this direction for advice. Besides, the therapist knew this child better than any other professional because she had worked directly with her for several years prior to the placement. After spending many weeks summoning the courage to share this intimate problem with the therapist, the family were devastated to receive such a hasty rebuff: 'I'm sorry I can't talk to you. That would be a betrayal of my relationship with the child.'

In this family's view, it would have been preferable if everyone working with the child had together devised a strategy for managing difficult behaviour. In this way they would all be trying to convey the same unambiguous messages to a very confused child.

When should therapy be provided? Occasionally a substitute family was convinced that the timing of therapy was inappropriate because the child was already struggling with too many conflicting emotions. Reflecting on a placement which had lasted a year, one adoptive mother of a boy aged 12 commented:

> During the past year this child has said to me so often 'I wish I was dead'. He is finding the need to change so hard . . . Over and above that there's therapy. The psychotherapist says that he needs therapy because it provides an outlet for his anger so that he doesn't let it out on me . . . but he gets angry because he has an appointment at a set time when someone is going to try to get him to open his chest of hurt – this padlocked box which is private – which he wants to keep out of reach of other people. His anger is stirred up and he remains angry for hours afterwards . . . Therapy is an intrusion. It disturbs him and unsettles the normal flow of events in the family.

At the time that this interview occurred, it happened that several therapy sessions which had been organized for this boy had to be cancelled. Privately, the adoptive mother acknowledged that the absence of therapy for a period of time had been a relief rather than a loss.

Sometimes, when a placement became very difficult or children began to exhibit extreme behavioural problems, social workers panicked. A frantic search was instigated for a therapist. In this way, the 'therapist' was frequently perceived as the magical solution. Minimal thought seemed to be given to the additional stress factor for children of introducing yet another adult at a point of such internal and external turmoil.

A striking feature of this study was how difficult substitute families found it to challenge the basis on which professionals worked. Even when all their instincts told them that what was being offered was not in the best interests of their foster or adoptive child, it was hard to criticize the experts. Families were liable to conclude that their intuitive assessment was much more likely to be flawed than the experts' diagnosis and treatment plan. Some shrugged their shoulders, doubtful if anyone would really listen even if they did attempt to voice their opinion:

> We could bring up our concerns. Would they be followed up? We have no titles after our name. We're just foster carers. If you want

professionals to listen, you have to use manoeuvres and tactics to make them believe that they brought up the issue themselves. That is the only way that you get any action.

After examining the opinions of families of children who did receive therapy, it is also important to learn from the experiences of those who had no access to it. Eight families expressed disappointment because therapy was not available to them. This was usually due to scarce or non-existent resources in a particular geographical area.

Just occasionally there was an expectation that a foster or adoptive family should assume total responsibility for undertaking therapy with the child themselves. This was an unsatisfactory situation which caused one foster mother to exclaim: 'That's no partnership. They either give you total responsibility or none at all. There's no opportunity to meet half-way.'

One single parent who had been pressurized to undertake therapy gave vent to her frustrations on the subject:

> Diane (11) has deep needs. I feel that she needs some kind of therapy and I need help to enable her to cope with it. I asked for it and I was told to do it myself. I have not got the space, equipment or knowledge. I have no training to fall back on. I'm frightened that I might make things worse . . . They treat me as if I have a degree in psychotherapy. It's very flattering that people think that I can do it, but the reality is that I can't.
>
> We're just like a car park for these children. Let's face it. No one would take their car to someone in a car park who knew nothing about the mechanical side of things and expect their car to come out tuned and in working order . . . We need a Union.

Families were certainly not advocating that they take on the therapist's role single-handed. Even the most experienced family rarely felt knowledgeable or self-assured enough to tackle this. Some families reached the conclusion that if they had been offered training, advice and ongoing consultation with a qualified therapist, their potential to help the child would have increased significantly.

Family therapy

Three foster families were offered family therapy run under the auspices of a psychiatrist. In one instance this offer did not materialize because the family were unable to meet essential criteria. One condition was that every family member was required to attend all therapy sessions. As the foster father worked shifts this was impossible. Many months later, the foster carers still felt angry about the manner in which they had been treated: 'Because we were unable to fit in with what was required, we were cut dead. That was it. No alternative was offered. Nothing else was recommended.'

The other two foster families who attended a series of sessions in family therapy complained also. Positive aspects of the experience were eclipsed by the fact that they felt that they were treated as if they were the original perpetrators of their foster children's abuse.

Group therapy

Ten children attended a series of group therapy sessions. In addition, two teenagers were offered this resource but resolutely declined to attend. These groups brought children who had been sexually abused together and were usually run by a psychologist or social worker. Once again, strong feelings were voiced because families felt so excluded. When children returned home 'swearing, bolshy and banging doors', families were left to surmise what exactly had stirred up such strong emotions.

One foster family whose teenage girl, Sue, attended group therapy on a regular basis received the following vague message through their social worker: 'The psychologist wants you to know that she is coming to a very difficult period in therapy.' When the family asked for the exact meaning of the phrase 'difficult period', their social worker acknowledged that she did not know herself and was therefore not in a position to enlighten them. Repeated requests by the family to meet the psychologist evoked no response, leaving the family angry and feeling totally devalued:

> The whole thing is like a brick wall. It blocks communication. Sue might talk to me about the problems of someone else in the group but she would never talk about herself . . . I don't agree with the way that they are handling it. They don't treat foster parents as equal colleagues. They treat you as someone beneath them. The psychologist is not interested in contacting me.

The aims of group therapy were rarely achieved. Usually children found the experience very stressful. Sometimes the group seemed to reactivate children's previous patterns of sexualized behaviour. Children who had a problem talking about their abuse tended to withdraw even further into themselves. In several cases behavioural problems became even more unmanageable. Some children had to be excluded from sessions; others withdrew before the full quota of group sessions was complete.

Three families attended a carers' group which ran in the same building at the same time as the children's group therapy sessions. The carers' group and the children's group functioned independently. In theory, this should have helped the foster carers to feel more involved in what was happening in the child's life. The reality, however, was that they had no idea about the content of therapy sessions for the child. Sometimes this had serious consequences. Very strong feelings were evoked for some children by therapy sessions. When children wanted to share sensitive information with their family immediately following a therapy session, it was not always easy for the family to know how to respond because they lacked basic information about the discussions that had precipitated the child's wish to talk. Crucial opportunities for communication were lost forever:

> One time on the way home in the train from a therapy session, Ann (6) started talking about the session. She had never managed to talk with us about her abuse before. It was clear that she was trying to say something about her past. I was in the dark. The problem was I had to guess at what had been discussed . . . then she clammed up completely.

Another practical problem emerged when the carers' and children's groups ran simultaneously. When a child's behaviour became unmanageable in the group, it was too easy to send an emergency message to the foster carer in an adjacent room. This was very distracting and hindered the potential usefulness of the carers' support group.

This chapter makes dismal and discouraging reading. If individual and group therapy are to be effective tools in adoption and fostering work, there is clearly a need to revise the philosophy underlying the work and to reconstruct the ground rules which govern its operation. In a previous chapter, consideration was given to the crucial importance of abused children being able to disclose to their adoptive and foster families; therapists' claims to have the exclusive right to tackle this sensitive subject often blocked communication between abused children and their foster or adoptive family. In this way the therapists were producing a whole new set of problems for children in placement. A further question arises: Why did social workers allow therapy work to develop in a manner which devalued and often excluded the contribution of substitute families? Social workers have a key role to play in helping therapists and substitute families to learn to communicate; to recognize and value each others' skills; and to work together within a clearly formulated and coherent plan for each child.

KEY ISSUES RELATED TO THERAPY

a) It is important to consider whether a model of therapy which places so much emphasis on an exclusive relationship between the child and the therapist is the most effective model to use in fostering and adoption work.

b) Therapists need to recognize the resourcefulness of substitute families and their potential to respond to every aspect of pain and hurt in the child's life. It is therefore unrealistic to expect substitute families to parent an abused child and to detach themselves from the sexual abuse aspect of the child's life.

c) It is just as unhelpful for a substitute family to be left to handle the complexities of sexual abuse alone as for therapists to feel that only they have the skills and techniques to manage this sensitive area. The reality is that a child who discloses within a therapy session may need to repeat this process within the security of the substitute family.

d) Communication is vital. Substitute families and therapists need to learn to respect each other's skills. This will never be achieved while the therapist's door remains closed to families.

e) Joint training between therapists and substitute families could be one means of helping each party to grapple with each others' perspective and to begin to establish relationships of mutual trust and understanding.

14　*Support: what is essential?*

The previous chapter addressed the issue of therapy as one potential source of support. This chapter examines other types of support, which were either available through families' own social networks or through professional services. How much personal understanding and practical assistance were relatives, friends and neighbours able to offer? Did other substitute families have a meaningful contribution to make to the placement? Were professional services adequate or inadequate?

INFORMAL NETWORKS OF SUPPORT THROUGH RELATIVES, FRIENDS AND NEIGHBOURS

The study indicates that remarkably little assistance was available to foster and adoptive families through relatives, friends and neighbours. Of course, there were isolated instances where an individual member of the extended family was a real 'lifeline'. In at least two situations an older married daughter, who lived locally, could almost have been considered to be in partnership with the foster carers because of the proportion of time which she spent caring for the abused child. In another case, a neighbour rescued a placement from the point of collapse by making a regular commitment to take the child out of the house for several hours daily. These were exceptions; the more general trend was for relatives, friends and neighbours to remain at a distance from the placement and offer very little practical or emotional support. Several factors seemed to influence this:

a) *The issue of confidentiality*: Foster and adoptive families often began the placement without telling their extended family or closest friends about the sexual abuse aspect of the case. Some families felt sworn to secrecy as a result of departmental directives or guidelines; others feared that any mention of the term 'sexual abuse' would create prejudice and destroy potentially good relationships. The result of this was that when problems immediately attributable to sexual abuse occurred it was difficult to talk frankly.

In quite a number of cases, the decision to remain taciturn about the sexual abuse aspect of the history did not last for long. When sexual incidents began to affect people close to the family, the silence had to be broken. In these circumstances, families often found themselves having to educate or support others rather than being recipients of help themselves.

b) *The intensity of behavioural problems*: Adoptive and foster families complained that it was often difficult for relatives and friends to understand or handle the difficulties occurring in the placement. Some withdrew quietly, recognizing that they were out of their depth; others were more vocal, insisting that the placement should be terminated.

c) *Fear of sexualized behaviour*: Some relatives and friends panicked at the first hint of sexualized behaviour. Handling this type of precocious behaviour was outside the experience of most people and could be intensely embarrassing. The child's normal appearance was not in harmony with such bizarre behaviour. Consequently, it was difficult for people to respond sympathetically. Some decided that it was easier to retreat rather than to remain in close contact with the family.

SUPPORT THROUGH OTHER FOSTER AND ADOPTIVE FAMILIES

Many of the 57 foster families in the study had contact with others experienced in fostering work. Twenty-six out of 57 (46 per cent) were regular members of a local foster carers group. For some this was a very significant source of support. The group provided an opportunity to release tensions and to compare notes about different methods of combating problem behaviour. Listening to others also created a more balanced perspective on current difficulties. When a support group was well established, every member of the group could rally round at a time of crisis:

When one of the girls accused my husband of sexual abuse, we felt completely 'out on a limb'. We were hurt but determined to continue fostering . . . We had no one to talk to. We couldn't talk to my mum, neighbours or friends . . . We had been members of the fostering group for five years. The whole group supported us. Someone from the group would telephone me every day. They were the only people we could talk to.

The usefulness of some groups extended far beyond talking. Two local groups had devised a system whereby individual members could provide childsitting or respite care for each other on a reciprocal basis. This met a crucial need for some families who were struggling with very complex placements.

Group support was not such a positive experience for every family. Some families felt isolated because they were the only ones tackling sexual abuse. Others described their group as too traditional and rigid:

I tended not to go to the support group. What I was doing was so different and so much more difficult. They would have been too shocked. You have to compromise with these kids. Another child I had was smoking cannabis. At the group I said that I would rather him smoke cannabis than drink and be violent. They were so shocked. I would hate to think how they would have reacted if I had talked about sexual abuse in the group.

Sometimes fear of breaching confidentiality blocked open discussion. At other times group members were too overwhelmed by their own problems to be able to listen effectively to others. Experienced families sometimes felt that they were putting more into the group than they were receiving in return.

Even if foster families derived minimal help from the group, they were usually able to establish a significant link with at least one other family. Some were in regular telephone contact, frequently listening and responding to each others' dilemmas. The Watt family described how access to another experienced foster carer at the time of disclosure was their 'life saver':

When the children were talking about what happened to them I had a terrible need to talk to someone. I felt so bad. If I had burst into tears with the kids, where would they have got their strength? When I turned to my foster friend I just sobbed uncontrollably. She would drop everything and listen. It was marvellous to have a 'listening ear'.

Others felt that in an emergency, their first telephone call would be to another foster family rather than to the emergency social services number.

In contrast to foster families, adoptive families had very few personal links with other experienced adopters. Only one agency ran a regular support group for adopters. Several adopters would have welcomed contact with another family with experience of sexual abuse, but they were at a loss to know exactly how to instigate these links themselves. A number of statutory and voluntary agencies failed to recognize the potential usefulness of this form of support for adopters.

RELEVANCE OF A SPECIALIST TELEPHONE HELPLINE

Some adoptive families requested access to a specialist telephone helpline in child sexual abuse. The fact that adoptive rather than foster families asked for this resource was probably because they often tended to feel more isolated. It was envisaged that this helpline would be run collaboratively by professionals with experience of working in the sphere of child sexual abuse and experienced foster and adoptive parents. The helpline would be used when difficulties occurred in the placement, or at a time of crisis.

PROFESSIONAL SUPPORT

Social work support

Of all the professionals concerned with the placement, social workers were in closest contact with foster and adoptive families. They were, therefore, in the best position to assess the families' need for support and to ensure that they either provided it directly themselves or enlisted other services as appropriate. Many families set out on the placement from a disadvantaged position. Too many had received minimal training or no training at all in sexual abuse. Consequently, they were having to assimilate the basic facts while simultaneously handling the demands of the placement. Another impediment was that families were frequently denied access to children's full background details. Before considering the question of support, it is important to stress that access to general facts about sexual abuse and to specific information about the particular child in placement are vital prerequisites to any adoption or fostering placement. Only when these conditions have been adequately fulfilled can support services be constructed on a sound foundation.

There was clear evidence that it was not only families who required access to information through training. Although insufficient time existed to talk directly to social workers about their perceived training needs, families reported that they felt inadequately supported when their social worker had limited knowledge and experience in this sphere of work. Dedication to the work could not compensate for a basic lack of knowledge:

> Our social worker was honest, understanding and she took time to listen but she was totally inexperienced in sexual abuse. We needed advice and reassurance, but the subject was new to the adoption officer. You need someone with experience who will guide you by saying 'If you get into this type of conversation, channel it this way'. If we had to handle it again, we would make sure we got a lot more information on the subject.

Social workers also needed to be prepared for the emotional impact associated with sexual abuse. Coming face to face with the stark reality of sexual abuse could be a devastating experience, not just for the foster or adoptive family but also for the professionals concerned. Some children in this study had been subjected to excessive abuse. Social workers could also be overwhelmed by feelings of revulsion. When this happened, families felt unsupported: 'Social workers were horrified. Horror took away the help we needed.'

The following aspects associated with parenting sexually abused children became apparent as foster and adoptive families described their experiences. Each one is worth considering because it has immediate implications for the social worker's role.

Key issues relevant to fostering or adopting sexually abused children	Implications for the social worker's role
a) The stressful nature of the task.	a) The need to invest time with the family.
b) The task involved reparenting rather than just parenting.	b) Families needed direction and guidance in their work.
c) Crises were liable to occur.	c) An easily accessible 24 hour emergency service was essential.

132

a) Stresses/need for social worker to invest time

Families parenting sexually abused children carried enormous tensions which they desperately needed to find an outlet for. It was vital that social workers invest time with families, listening and absorbing the painful feelings which could so easily break out in all directions and completely destroy the placement: 'I feel like a punch bag. The best help is to be listened to.'

Some social services departments were experimenting with the idea of one worker supporting several foster families together through group meetings rather than the time consuming procedure of every family being visited by an individual social worker. From social services' viewpoint there were many economic advantages associated with group support. Foster families were less impressed by what such a system had to offer them. They unanimously agreed that, when they were confronting the day-to-day demands of caring for an abused child, their need was best met by their social worker visiting them regularly at home. This provided an opportunity for them to ventilate strong feelings, make sense of events and to plan strategies for coping in the future. The following features were essential to ensure that this type of support was effective:

  i) it needed to be built into the framework of support from the outset of the placement;
 ii) contact with the social worker required to be on a regular basis.

Some social workers who were providing this type of consistent service received effusive praise from families. They were perceived as the 'backbone' of the placement. Their role was so important that it made the difference between the placement succeeding or failing.

Some agencies tried to operate a more 'open door' policy, whereby the onus was placed on families' shoulders to call for help when this became essential. This system failed abysmally; families were ambivalent about calling on the services of overworked social workers. Privately, they reasoned that they should be able to manage without professional assistance. Besides, they thought that there must be many more needy cases than their own. The result was that minor difficulties often escalated to crisis proportions before the family plucked up the courage to make that essential telephone call.

When the relationship between the social worker and the family was poorly defined, families could spend days trying to get access to the right person:

> Social workers are not positive enough. They rush in and out and they don't have enough time for you. Often they're too professional. You ring up and you never get them. 'I'm sorry – they're on a Course for two days.' Then you ring again when they're due back. 'Oh, they're on two days' leave now.' By the time the social worker appears, the minor problem is a major one.

The model in fostering work which worked best was for two social workers to be involved: one representing the child's needs and the other supporting the family. In some areas, attempts were made to short-circuit this procedure by allocating one social worker for both parties. Foster families always felt disadvantaged when they did not have a link worker specially allocated to help them.

There were special times of difficulty when additional social work time needed to be allocated to the family:

i) at the time of disclosure;
ii) when the foster or adoptive family was required to provide evidence in court;
iii) at the time when an allegation was made against the family;
iv) when the abused child's behaviour was completely out of control.

In the case of one agency an unusual phenomenon was reported; families complained that social workers were allocating too much time to them:

> The social worker has come once a week. He has reviewed everything that has happened to the foster children each week. I usually feel angry when he goes away. We've had too much support. It's been very time consuming. Every Tuesday we take the children 40 miles for therapy. Every Thursday the social worker comes. Our view is that the children are normal. The social worker's view is 'The children are different. They have to learn to be different'. Of course the social worker himself suffered as a child. I think all his work is coloured by that.

Similar sentiments were expressed by an adoptive family working with the same agency:

> The older boy says 'Why does the social worker need to come. I'm just going to tell her to "shoo off".' We can't see the sense of all the work. We feel that it is all a waste of time. What she does doesn't seem to show. The other day she said 'I have a couple of years' work ahead with the boys' . . . to think of someone coming into the house every week in two years' time! When the social worker disappears, I say to my wife

'Let what she says in one ear and out the other – and let's just carry on'.

Although these examples are rather exceptional, they do point to the need for support to be negotiated and re-negotiated with the foster or adoptive family so that the service provided coincides with families' real needs.

b) Re-parenting task/need for direction and guidance

Foster and adoptive families often had to engage in an active rather than a passive parenting task. Many children had learned unacceptable patterns of sexual behaviour which required to be radically transformed. One of the most complex tasks facing families was re-educating children about appropriate and inappropriate family relationships. There was often a professional assumption that foster and adoptive families had an innate ability to engage in this difficult re-parenting task. Even the most experienced families often felt frustrated because they were left to drift without adequate professional guidance:

> Nobody ever gave us direction. People weren't experienced enough. They used to say 'We're learning together'. They admit that they're doing all their learning from our foster girl . . . We had one meeting with one of the top men from social services when we were going through a crisis. He said an interesting thing – 'Have you thought of confronting her with what she's doing? It's important to confront her so that she understands what she's doing.' I found that helpful. It made me wonder how many more gems of knowledge are there which no one thought to tell us.

Some families had the capacity to do very skilled direct work with abused children. Even the most talented readily acknowledged that they needed regular supervision and consultation:

> The 14-year-old girl we have now has been with us since April 1987. She was sexually abused by her step-father when she was two to four years. I have done a lot of direct work with her with the help and supervision of my specialist link worker (now alas no longer employed by the same social services department). I have managed through my work to release this girl from her 'frozen' state and to begin to accept cuddles.
> I need constant supervision of my work – someone to talk to – someone with ideas – someone to reassure and guide me – to help me to

know how far to go. Since my specialist worker has left, there's been no input. We've all suffered. I've been left to my own devices. Attempts have been made to find someone locally but so far without success.

Families also complained that their social worker was often at a loss to know how to help them undertake sex education with an abused child. This was a difficult area because the child had often grown to accept inappropriate relationships as the norm. Families often felt disappointed because they were left to muddle their way through this difficult area rather than receiving adequate guidance and direction.

c) Crises/need for a 24-hour service

This was not a predictable area of work which could be easily contained within the hours of 9 a.m. to 5 p.m. Crises were common and there was a vital need for a 24-hour service which was easily accessible. As many as 45 out of 66 families (68 per cent) required help in an emergency outside normal office hours. Reasons for this included a child absconding; a birth parent threatening to remove a child; death of a close relative; hospitalization of a child; a further incident of physical or sexual abuse; a suicide attempt; a child out of control; an adoptive family feeling unable to withstand the demands of the placement; and a final crisis leading to disruption.

Some families had difficulty getting access to help when these crises occurred. Contacting the normal out-of-hours emergency service run by local social services departments was fraught with difficulty. The quality of support failed to fulfil families' needs and frequently added another pressure. There were numerous complaints about the service being slow, and of social workers lacking specialist knowledge and skill. Another frustration was having to relate the abused child's complex case history all over again to a total stranger:

There's very little help after 5.30 p.m. There is an emergency service but it's very complicated. If at 11.30 p.m. the child comes out on to the landing hysterical, there is no one to help. You have to work by instinct . . . I rang once. I needed help immediately. It took two to three hours for anyone to come. Help over the phone is no help. You can get your own help that way. When you've had a night-time emergency and you ring the department, the next day they say 'Oh, we didn't know anything about it'. It makes you wonder 'How emergency is emergency?'

In another case where a single parent had reached breaking point, the emergency service provided seemed to encourage the placement towards collapse:

> When I collapsed I was in no fit state to search for an emergency number. I remembered that the social worker had said 'If you're totally stuck, ring the police number'. The police switchboard didn't know what I wanted. Eventually I got through to the Emergency Social Work number, and I got this secretary. I told her my story. She thought that it was so funny that she went into hysterics. I could hear her laughing with her colleagues and repeating the story to them while I was hanging on the other end of the phone.
>
> At last I got through to the social worker. I just kept saying 'I'm desperate – I need a break'. She kept telling me to give up. Then she kept asking 'Do you love him? If you love him why on earth do you want a break? Then she told me to think about it and she would ring back later. She came back on with the same question 'What do you want a rest for if you love him?' Eventually I slammed the phone down. It was a waste of time talking to her.

These problems were largely overcome when families had access to their social worker's home telephone number for emergency purposes. In fact, some families were able to defer making that crucial telephone call until the next morning because they felt reassured by the knowledge that they could contact their own social worker at any stage throughout the night.

The gender of the social worker providing support

Consideration should always be given to whether the gender of the social worker supporting the placement may be hindering an adoptive or foster family from openly discussing problems which are affecting the placement. In one fostering placement, the children's history of sexual abuse became so repugnant to the foster mother that she found it difficult to retain a sexual relationship with her husband. At the same time, she found it impossible to talk with her male social worker about this intimate aspect of her life. In another adoption placement, the abused child's close relationship with the adoptive father became a source of jealousy to the adoptive mother. Stage by stage, the adopters' own relationship deteriorated, including their sex life. Trapped by feelings of guilt and isolation, the adoptive mother felt that she could not begin to discuss what was happening with her male social worker. Although this study does not highlight similar issues in relation to foster and adoptive fathers, it is not difficult to envisage that parallel situations may occur when men may find it too difficult to talk with a female social worker. While it would be unhelpful to make a generalized statement on this subject, the issue of gender is an important one which should not be ignored in an area of work which is likely to make an impact on sexual feelings and relationships.

Access to specialist knowledge in child sexual abuse

'Where are the experts with specialist and definitive knowledge in child sexual abuse?' This was a question raised by a number of foster and adoptive families, who often found themselves surrounded by professional uncertainties and disagreements concerning sexually abused children. In the previous chapter, reference was made to unresolved debates about 'Which children need therapy?', 'When is therapy likely to be most effective?' Another question which particularly preoccupied adopters concerned the longer term effects of sexual abuse: 'What scars are children liable to carry into adolescence and adulthood?' Others wondered about the long term prospects for children who suffered sexual abuse when they were still at a pre-verbal stage of development. These were just some themes on which professional opinions seemed to be speculative rather than authoritative.

Twenty-two out of 66 (33 per cent) felt that they required much more specialist knowledge than they were offered. There were frustrations associated with working in a relatively new field, which despite receiving so much publicity often lacked a solid factual base. Most families preferred to learn through access to people with specialist knowledge and understanding rather than through literature, yet it was often difficult to get access to someone with professional competence in this field. Those who did search for books often expressed disappointment. Current literature was perceived as too technical, rather abstract and not immediately relevant to adoption and fostering.

Families often found themselves dependent on their own day-to-day experiences as the most effective source of learning. Many acknowledged that this was an inadequate basis from which to attempt to help a traumatised child. Several were convinced that they could have offered the child more if they had had easier access to specialist knowledge.

Advice from a child psychologist about modifying difficult behaviour

Foster and adoptive families frequently struggled with anti-social, aggressive or sexualized behaviour. Very occasionally, a family's need for specialist help through a psychologist was recognized immediately and built in from the outset of the placement. One adoptive family who was offered this service at the beginning of their placement enthused about it: 'Four-year-old Danny was very aggressive and he used to bite badly. Programmes were worked out by the psychologist to help him calm down. After five weeks, we began to see a difference. The programme began to take effect.'

This type of early intervention was certainly not the norm. It was much more common for families to struggle with difficult behaviour over a protracted period single-handedly. After resorting to a repertoire of trial and error approaches, some complained of total exhaustion and exasperation. It was easy for feelings of optimism to wane as the same problem continued to dominate family life. Some families were at a loss to know where to turn for advice. The following example illustrates how the child's problem could disturb everyone in the family unless a consistent method of tackling it could be devised:

Susie (four years) was so clingy to my husband. She would hang on to his legs the minute he walked in the door. When he went to the toilet she would follow him and wait outside the door. When he sat down he would plonk herself on his lap. Was it because she had never had a father figure or was she trying to arouse him? After six months the atmosphere in our family had changed completely. I needed help if we were ever going to get back to normal, but there was nowhere to turn . . . It just so happened that I had an appointment to go and see a child psychologist about another placement. I grasped my chance and poured my worries out to her. She suggested that we used the following words with Susie: 'GIVE DADDY BREATHING SPACE'. I used them. My husband used them. The other kids used them. The words were like magic. It took her about a week to understand. She learned that she could cuddle my husband, go away and that he would still be there when she came back later.

This snippet of advice may have seemed minor to the psychologist. It was crucial for the family and created a real turning point in the placement. This family considered themselves to be fortunate because they had gained access to a psychologist. They were keen to point out, however, that this meeting had occurred by a happy coincidence rather than as a result of careful professional planning.

Others were less fortunate. Even when a family and social worker had together identified a psychologist as a key person to help them, there was no guarantee that they would get immediate access to this person: 'The help is there but everyone is too busy. We have had to wait for months and months to get an appointment with a psychologist to give us advice on how to proceed.'

Towards the conclusion of the research interview all the families were asked 'Have you at any stage ever looked for any particular type of help in relation to a sexually abused child and been unable to find it?' Several commented in general terms on the need for someone to guide them through a programme for modifying behaviour. Others identified a child psychologist as the most appropriate person to help them with this, and felt aggrieved because they were denied this service:

> I desperately needed to learn how to modify and control difficult behaviour. I used to be tearing my hair out and searching through a book entitled 'The A–Z of Behavioural Problems' for any idea or insight I could get. I needed far more than that. At one point I became physically ill with the emotional strain . . . They treat you as if you have a degree in Psychology and as if you know exactly what to do.

The relevance of respite care

Figure 11 Use of respite care

Families who used respite care	Families who would have liked to use respite care if it had been available	Families who did not wish to use respite care
13	12	41

Total: 66

Twenty-five out of 66 (38 per cent) either used or would have liked to have used respite care. Of these, thirteen families had had access to some form of family based or residential respite care scheme. Those who had used this resource were usually very enthusiastic about its value. Frequently respite care was one of the key resources which they felt enabled them to tolerate the demands of the placement. One foster family commented 'Respite was our "safety valve"'. Several felt that they would have used respite care more often if this had been feasible. Sometimes the distance factor between the respite family and the adoptive or foster family made this quite impractical. Some yearned for a suitable resource in their immediate locality. Occasionally the experience of using family based respite care was soured by a sexual incident occurring between the abused child and one of the other children in the respite family.

In five cases, respite was first introduced at a point of crisis when the family were feeling totally overwhelmed by the demands of the placement. This type of emergency planning was far from ideal for the abused child, the foster or the adoptive family or the social worker who often had to instigate a frantic search for some type of respite facility either inside or outside the region.

Twelve families were denied access to respite care despite the fact that they would have warmly welcomed this type of help. Some who asked for it at the outset of the placement found their request ignored. Adoptive families were much less likely to be offered this facility than foster families. There seemed to be an inbuilt assumption that adoption could be equated with coping independently. Some families complained that no one ever mentioned respite care to them, so they were totally unaware of its existence. Perhaps the most frustrated families were those who were offered respite care by their social worker in an abstract manner, at the point of planning the placement, but later when they made a specific request for it they quickly discovered that the notion could not be translated into reality. One disillusioned foster mother exclaimed: 'I discovered that the idea of respite care only existed in the social worker's head.'

Another adoptive father felt that their inordinate level of stress should have been obvious to their social worker and their urgent need for respite care acknowledged:

> We lived with an unacceptable level of stress. The kind of respite which we were offered was like someone saying to us 'Shall I help you fix your car?' and then walking away. If they had wanted to help, they should have recognized our stress and been on hand with it.

Some of the 41 families who responded to the question 'Would you have benefited from having respite care available to you?' with a categorical 'No' were keen to explain their reasons for this answer. Although many felt a need for a period of respite for themselves, they worried that children would interpret any breach in their relationship as a further rejection: 'It would have harmed her. She had already been rejected. She needed to know whatever I throw at them, they will hold on.' Others felt that the idea of respite care was 'pie in the sky'. They were extremely sceptical that anyone existed who could handle their placement effectively.

Seven families preferred to use their extended family rather than any formal respite care scheme. Family members who were most useful often had specialist experience of fostering themselves or had worked at some stage with children with special needs. Other substitutes for respite care which some families preferred to use were a local club; extra nursery time being provided when behavioural problems became unmanageable; a regular commitment from a volunteer to take a child out for several hours weekly; and teenagers being able to obtain part-time employment during evenings or weekends.

If respite care schemes had been more easily accessible and if more careful planning had occurred at an earlier stage in relation to certain families' need for this resource, some of the difficulties that emerged in this study could have been lessened. It is unrealistic for local authority departments and voluntary agencies to expect foster and adoptive families to take on such a difficult task without ensuring that respite care is at least available. The decision to use or to decline to use this resource can then be made by each family. Adoption placements are as likely to require some type of respite provision as foster placements and their needs should not be overlooked.

Partnership between substitute families and professionals: fact or fiction?

The notion of partnership between professionals and substitute families is easier to endorse in theory than to put into practice. One particular area in which the concept of partnership was noticeably absent was when families were excluded from important reviews and case conferences. This affected a small group of six out of 66 families (nine per cent) who found themselves excluded from crucial decision-making about the child in their care. Some found it difficult to remain calm as they alluded to this: 'It's totally appalling that they don't invite us . . . All the disclosure work took place in this house but we were still not invited.'

Sometimes families were not only excluded from meetings but also denied information about crucial case conference decisions, which had far reaching consequences for the child and themselves. The worst example of this concerned prospective adopters. David (8) was placed with a family on the clear understanding that access to his mother would continue. David wanted this contact and the adopters were also convinced that it was in his best interests. Several weeks into the placement, the adopters were alarmed to discover that crucial decisions about access had been overturned at a case conference on the day that David had moved to them. The most disconcerting element was that nobody had talked to David about altering the original plan, nor had any dialogue occurred between the adopters and the social services department responsible for David. Eventually this placement disrupted. Confusion about access was one of a larger number of factors which militated against the success of the placement.

Sixty out of 66 families (90 per cent) were permitted to attend reviews and case conferences. Forty-two out of the 60 (64 per cent) felt very positively about this experience. Comments like 'We were treated like Royalty' or 'We were totally involved' were common. Several very experienced families referred to how much professional attitudes towards adoptive and foster families had improved in their local area.

The remaining 18 out of 60 families (30 per cent) recorded a different story. They felt 'belittled' and disillusioned with the entire system. Several complained that their 'viewpoint was brushed aside' or that the content of their written reports was too readily dismissed. Two families who were allowed to attend case conferences were not permitted to read the minutes of the meeting, which were circulated to professionals only. One foster carer described the humiliation which she experienced when she attended an important case conference and was treated as an 'outsider': 'I felt two inches tall. It was "them" and "us". The team leader announced "I have a report here but I can't read it because it can't be discussed with someone in this room owing to confidentiality".'

This section raises the question 'What exactly is the status of foster carers and adopters?' Much more work requires to be undertaken by professionals in clarifying the working relationships, responsibilities and status of substitute carers.

WORKING ACROSS PROFESSIONAL BOUNDARIES

Social workers do not hold a monopoly of knowledge about child sexual abuse. Other professionals have a crucial role to play in helping abused children. Due to time constraints, it was not possible to study the roles and functions of each professional discipline in detail. However, each family was asked about the helpfulness or unhelpfulness of all professionals with whom they came into contact throughout the placement. Teaching staff, police involved mainly at the point of disclosure, and different members of the medical profession were mentioned frequently.

Working with schools

Considerable confusion surrounded the question 'Should the school know about sexual abuse?' Especially in adoption placements, it was a contentious issue who should make the decision about informing or not informing the school about the child's history of abuse. Should responsibility lie with the agency responsible for the placement or should the family make the ultimate decision? What should happen when the social worker and family are unable to agree on this matter? Some adopters spent sleepless nights worrying about questions like: If I tell the school will my child be stigmatized for life? Of course there were implications associated with not telling also. Adopters feared that their silence might be open to misinterpretation, especially if their child decided to confide in a teacher. Alternatively, a child's words or drawings might be misconstrued: 'Margaret (7) used to speak about "old dad" and "new dad". One day the teacher told me that she did a drawing and wrote "Dad's peanuts". "Oh gosh" I thought. "What if she says *my dad* and they think that it is my husband?"'

There were wide variations in foster and adoptive families' attitudes towards the helpfulness or unhelpfulness of schools. Comments ranged from 'The school was magnificent', 'I'd give top marks to the school' to the other extreme of 'The school was disastrous', 'They could not begin to understand'. Even within a particular school, staff attitudes could vary very considerably. Some teachers wanted to dismiss the idea of sexual abuse as a fabrication or exaggeration, especially when the alleged perpetrator was a close member of the child's immediate family. Others took the issue very seriously and responded in a sensitive and balanced manner. Families often identified individual members of staff who had been understanding and made comparisons with others: 'The Art teacher and the Technical Drawing teacher were marvellous. They supported us. The others were dreadful.'

Good communication between the substitute family and the school was essential. Frequently sexual incidents occurred at school between the abused child and other children or adults. These episodes required sensitive handling at home and at school. New worries emerged when the class was undertaking a programme of sex education. Some families who had remained silent on the subject of sexual abuse felt compelled to approach the school at this point.

Families who were adopting or fostering for the first time often assumed that communication between themselves and the school would evolve automatically. They were often surprised and frustrated to discover how much time and energy needed to be spent constructing meaningful relationships with school staff. This was essential if teachers and substitute parents were to adopt a consistent approach towards the child's special needs.

A common complaint was that teachers tended to be over- sympathetic. One family criticized the teacher for regularly taking their eight-year-old foster girl on her knee and treating her as a baby. Another commented: 'Feelings of pity took over and they did not see the full picture.'

Occasionally an abused child seemed to have two personalities, one evident in the classroom, the other apparent only in the home. Some children reserved their worst behaviour for those closest to them. When the family was bearing the brunt of uncontrollable outbursts from the child, the school might not necessarily be experiencing similar problems; there were instances when the same child was subdued and totally conforming to every classroom rule. Under these circumstances it was easy for the school to allege that the family's incompetent handling of the child must be the root cause of the child's level of disturbance.

Sometimes the family and the school had opposing ideas about the level of supervision which an abused child might require. Foster and adoptive families were accused of 'going over the top' and being 'overprotective': 'The school was a disaster. They were not with me. They used to say to me "Why don't you treat her like a normal 12-year-old?" They were not up to her. The headteacher had no idea. The school was a big let down.'

In some instances the abused child's behaviour was totally unmanageable at school. Expulsions occurred, often because of uncontrollable behaviour. Some schools that had no previous experience of integrating 'hard to place' children acknowledged that they were completely out of their depth.

The process of learning to work effectively with schools can be an enormous pressure for foster and adoptive families of sexually abused children. This issue needs to be addressed during preparation of substitute families. Teachers also require relevant training if they are to respond appropriately to the needs of sexually abused children and their substitute families.

Working with the police

Frequently, police involvement occurred at the stage of disclosure when evidence was being collated for the purposes of prosecution. Foster and adoptive families' attitudes to police intervention were predominantly positive. Police were described as sensitive and understanding. Several families made positive comments about the fact that the policeman or woman did not usually wear uniform. They felt that this was less intimidating for children, who were often frightened because previous contact with officialdom had occurred at some of the most distressing periods in their lives.

In a number of situations, police did have special problems communicating with abused children. Two factors appeared consistently in situations where these difficulties occurred. Firstly, if the child was of pre-school age or a slow learner verbal communication was difficult for the child.

Secondly, if the child's experience of abuse did not fit into a stereotype. For example, one girl who made no secret of the fact that her experience of sexual abuse had been pleasurable left the police completely bewildered as she bombarded them with her story of abuse in an excited voice. They had arrived at the house expecting to meet a distressed child and were astounded by her reaction.

Working with the medical profession

Family doctor

Occasionally the family doctor was closely involved in the sexual abuse aspect of the child's life. Sometimes doctors were highly commended: 'The doctor was marvellous. He was very sympathetic and sensitive to Elaine. She had to have a medical and he took great care not to do anything that would make her feel uncomfortable. She even allowed him to carry out an internal.'

Others were less impressed with the quality of professional services which they received. One foster carer who thought that she should forewarn the family doctor of her foster girl's vulnerability due to sexual abuse was quickly rebuffed: 'I tried to talk to the G.P. I made an appointment. When I said that I wanted to talk with him about the children's history of sexual abuse he quickly said "That will be totally unnecessary".'

Psychiatrist

Psychiatrists had a much higher profile in this study than the family doctor. Twenty-eight out of 66 families (42 per cent) had contact with a psychiatrist at some stage during the placement. In some cases a meeting occurred when a psychiatric assessment of the child was being under-taken. In other situations, the family were offered the opportunity to consult a psychiatrist about general issues concerning sexually abused children or about their specific child. These appointments were either recommended by the social worker or requested by the family them-selves. A number of families grasped this opportunity as a means of obtaining additional specialist knowledge about sexually abused children.

Twelve out of 28 families (43 per cent) found contact with the psychiatrist helpful, although some did acknowledge that sitting face to face with a psychiatrist could be a daunting experience. It was difficult to derive maximum benefit from the interview because they felt so intimidated: 'He was so professional. You felt that you couldn't say "Good morning" in case he would be interpreting it. After a while you could see that he was human.'

Families mentioned the following benefits associated with these interviews:

a) their knowledge about sexually abused children was enhanced;
b) they gained fresh insights into their particular child's difficulties;
c) they felt more confident about their method of tackling a specific problem after being reassured by the psychiatrist that they were approaching it appropriately.

Several warmly welcomed the option to return for further advice and consultation in the future if this proved to be necessary.

Sixteen out of the 28 (57 per cent) presented a much gloomier picture. Some felt that they were not given adequate time by the psychiatrist. In instances where the psychiatrist had known the child previously, some families were disappointed to encounter an immediate resistance towards sharing information openly with them. An additional dimension was that some families felt that they were automatically treated as if they were the original perpetrators of child abuse. Perhaps the most disconcerting aspect was when families sought advice about the future for children who had been sexually abused as babies or toddlers. Several found their enquiry brushed aside with the comment 'She'll forget'. In each instance the family's ongoing experience of caring for the child was sufficient to convince them that this advice was misguided.

It was not only access to a psychiatrist that was important but also the timing of this intervention. This type of specialist advice was too frequently introduced only at a point of crisis. One family who were offered a consultation when their placement was threatening to disrupt found that this resource was quickly withdrawn when the crisis passed. Another family who were enthusiastic about what they had learned through access to a psychiatrist regretted that the appointment arrived too late to avert disruption.

One foster carer dissolved into tears as she commented: 'The only way that you can get any specialist help in this area is by manufacturing a crisis.'

THE VITAL IMPORTANCE OF COLLABORATIVE WORKING

Poor communication between professionals and between agencies undermined placements. Abused children were sometimes caught up in an unnecessary web of professional distrust:

> Too many people were involved and they were all pulling the kid in different directions.
>
> The school didn't agree with social services. They didn't let anyone know what they were doing. The education welfare officer didn't agree with the school and he started having secrets with 15-year-old Lorraine. Lorraine was going home to the house where her abuser lived during her lunch break. The school knew about it but decided not to mention it. Everyone was doing their own little bit and the kid was caught in the middle.

Sometimes the family found it hard to give the child their undivided attention because professional disagreements imposed themselves on the placement and distracted them from their central task. The following example concerned an adoption placement made by a voluntary agency which began in a straightforward manner. Three months after placement, sexual abuse emerged as an unexpected factor; suddenly, the entire climate changed. Small informal case conferences became large unwieldy gatherings. A host of so-called 'experts' emerged at the first mention of the term 'sexual abuse'. Under these circumstances, it was only too easy for the children's needs to become submerged beneath professional disputes and rivalries, and for the family to feel totally overwhelmed:

> There were about 15 to 18 people at meetings. They were not always the same people and they were always wrangling between themselves. There were tensions between the Homefinding section and the Children's section. These tensions became an issue for us. We should

have been released from that. It got to the point where you felt that if the boys told you anything that it was simpler to keep quiet about it. You knew that if you told it would become a big drama and everything would get blown out of all proportion. The information had to be passed on to so many people. The management of it all was so poor. If we had not been experienced I don't think that the placement would have survived. There were too many things affecting the placement. At times we felt that we were carrying the professionals as well as the boys. I used to think 'Oh please give me peace to parent the boys'.

In theory, everyone knows that mutual trust, co-ordinated planning and effective communication are essential hallmarks of all fostering and adoption placements. Applying these principles becomes even more difficult in an emotive area like sexual abuse, which is inseparable from feelings of guilt, the tendency to attribute blame and a basic distrust of others. Barriers to working on an interdisciplinary basis require to be addressed and re-addressed so that they do not jeopardize placements.

KEY ISSUES RELATED TO SUPPORT

Fundamental requirements

Training:

a) Basic training in child sexual abuse.
b) Ongoing in-service training in child sexual abuse.

Background information:

Comprehensive background information about the child in placement – including full details about the child's history of sexual abuse.

Important aspects

Gender of social worker:

It is important to consider whether the gender of the social worker is hindering or facilitating communication about key issues affecting the placement. This is particularly necessary when aspects of people's own sexuality and sexual relationships begin to affect the placement.

149

Timing:

The timing of introducing support services is important. Support services should not be crisis-orientated.

The inter-disciplinary aspect:

Co-operative working and planning between professionals from different disciplines and between professionals and families is vital.

Social work support

What?

a) Home visits from a social worker during placement to provide:
   i) a listening ear;
   ii) direction in relation to:
      – the task of re-parenting;
      – sex education for the abused child.
b) A 24-hour emergency service.

When?

a) On a regular basis.
b) Inbuilt from the outset of the placement.

How?

Degree of contact to be negotiated with the family.

Support through other substitute families

a) The potential usefulness of links with other substitute families should be maximized.
b) Social workers may be required to create these links especially for adopters. Issues of confidentiality may make it difficult for them to locate other adopters themselves.

Other professional supports

a) Easy access to professionals with knowledge and experience in child sexual abuse.

b)* Access to a child psychologist to advise or design programmes for modifying anti-social, aggressive or sexualized behaviour.

c)* Respite care.

d) Therapy (programmes to be designed in liaison with the substitute family and as a co-ordinated part of a total support service available to abused children).

* Every family may not choose to use b) and c). If they are available, the family can decide themselves whether to accept or reject the service.

15 Summary and conclusions

The fact that any child requiring substitute family care in Britain today may have been sexually abused has immediate implications for all foster and adoptive families. It may not always be apparent that sexual abuse is a factor in a child's background at the point of placement. Sometimes it is only within the security of a foster or adoptive family that children may feel able to divulge such sensitive secrets from their past. It is, therefore, essential that every substitute family is knowledgeable about the reality of sexual abuse, sensitive to its implications and aware that they may find themselves unexpectedly parenting a sexually abused child.

Training in child sexual abuse for foster and adoptive families is not an optional extra: it is crucial. Although many families in this study did manage to undertake this work without prior training, they were the first to acknowledge that lack of information and self-doubt placed both themselves and the abused child in a disadvantaged position. A commitment to training on the part of social services departments and voluntary agencies is, therefore, essential. This will inevitably require an investment of financial resources and staff time.

Training is relevant for highly experienced substitute families as well as the less experienced. Ongoing opportunities for training helped families recognize their own strengths and weaknesses, review their own attitudes to sexual abuse, derive fresh insights into how they might tackle problematical behaviour, and keep in touch with new developments in the study of sexual abuse. The model used for training social workers can readily be applied to foster and adoptive families. A basic training provides individuals with a foundation of knowledge, but there is endless scope to continue to build on that framework.

SEXUAL ABUSE: A FACTOR IN THE CARER'S BACKGROUND

It is important to consider that people who apply to foster or adopt children may themselves have a hidden history of sexual abuse. This issue should, therefore, be addressed in all fostering and adoption applications. People with personal histories of sexual abuse need to have the opportunity to face the reality of their own abuse and to be aware of their own vulnerability. The experience of parenting a sexually abused child is likely to reactivate painful feelings from the past. The fact that someone has suffered sexual abuse should not lead to instant panic on the part of the professionals. Each situation needs to be fully explored; in some cases a history of abuse may be a very positive factor motivating people to help abused children. The study indicates that it is feasible for some abused carers and abused children to live together in such a way that each manages to derive strength and help through interacting with the other.

Victims of abuse who decide to foster or adopt may feel 'full to the brim' with anger towards the child's abuser. It is only too easy for unresolved personal feelings of anger, injustice and even repugnance to become inextricably linked with feelings towards the child's abuser. Encouraging traumatized children to understand and grapple with their past is an important function for any foster and adoptive family. Carers who have been abused themselves may find it difficult to tackle this sensitive area and are likely to need help to unravel the feelings which belong to their own past and those which relate to the child's immediate situation. Those who feel able to meet the child's abuser face to face may find some of their overwhelmingly negative attitudes diminished through this process.

BACKGROUND INFORMATION

When professionals are aware that sexual abuse is a factor in any child's background, it is vital that this information is shared openly with the foster and adoptive family. It is not only a basic statement concerning sexual abuse which families need to obtain but also the fullest possible detail about:

– Who abused?
– What type of abuse occurred?
– When did it happen?
– Where did it happen?

The more detailed information which families receive, the more adequately equipped they will be to handle the day-to-day demands of the placement.

A good partnership between professionals and substitute families is noticeably lacking when background reports are concealed under the guise of 'confidentiality'. In particular, this study highlighted the unhelpful approach of therapists towards sharing information. This had an undermining effect on those stuggling with the day-to-day care of very difficult children. Ultimately, abused children and their foster or adoptive families are seriously disadvantaged when unnecessary blanks exist in the child's background history.

When the foster or adoptive family are informed that the background information which they receive is confidential, they need a clear and realistic definition of the meaning of this term. Some families who took part in this study felt compelled to breach departmental rules about confidentiality when sexual incidents occurred, or seemed to loom on the horizon, with people outside the family. Although a number felt guilty about taking this step, they admitted that remaining silent would merely have exacerbated the child's problems. While it is, of course, expedient to safeguard children's interests by recognizing the importance of confidentiality, it is easy to carry this issue to an extreme and to create extra problems for the abused child and the substitute family. It is essential that professionals and substitute families together reach a consensus on a workable definition of the term 'confidentiality'.

PREPARATION FOR THE REALITY OF CARING FOR A SEXUALLY ABUSED CHILD

Foster and adoptive families require preparation for the whole range of difficulties which they are likely to encounter with sexually abused children. Those who already have experience of caring for 'hard to place' children may be familiar with the problems commonly associated with deprivation. Lying, stealing, eneuresis, encopresis, withdrawal, aggressive behaviour, self-mutilation and rejection of one parent are just a few examples. It is not surprising to discover all these features appearing throughout this study, after all, sexual abuse is likely to be one of a multiplicity of factors which has made an impact on children's lives. Other forms of neglect such as physical abuse, inadequate parenting and constant moves in and out of care will have taken their toll also.

Over and above these problems are the complications which occur because of the abused child's sexual history. Handling everyday difficulties takes on a new level of complexity because any form of physical contact can easily be misconstrued by the abused child as a cue for a sexual relationship. Non-verbal signs which are readily understood by other family members may mean something totally inappropriate to the highly sexualized child.

Families need to be prepared for the fact that an abused child may try to touch their bodies in a sexual manner. It is important that people spend time in advance of the placement reflecting on ways of managing this behaviour. The impact of sexual touching is liable to be more stressful than people have anticipated. The feelings of powerlessness associated with this experience were summed up by several in the words: 'I felt like I was being abused myself.'

Parenting an abused child is likely to impinge on people's own sexuality. Individuals may find themselves face to face with unexpected sexual feelings. Weaknesses in a couple's sex life may be exposed. Even very young children can present a major threat on a sexual level to close adult relationships. Acknowledging the personal pain associated with this may be difficult for the person most intimately affected. Caring for a sexually abused child can, therefore, be a very distressing task, charged with personal emotion. There is a constant risk of the child disturbing some of the most sensitive and intimate aspects of family relationships.

An awareness of the connection between eating problems and sexual abuse is important. In particular, children who have experienced oral sex may be repelled by foods such as sausages or bananas touching their mouths because of their resemblance in shape to a penis. Foods which are similar in texture to semen may also be detested.

Abused children may recoil from touching their genitals. Daily routines like washing and bathing may be particularly difficult, not because of obstinacy but rather as an immediate consequence of sexual abuse.

Another taxing feature of daily life which appeared again and again in this study was the child's tendency to dominate everyone. Attempts by girls to usurp the foster or adoptive mother's role in the household could easily disturb the equilibrium of family life. Children who have frequently been so powerless in an abusive relationship may find it difficult to handle control appropriately within an ordinary family.

Abused children's behaviour may be totally erratic. One minute the child may behave like a toddler, the next moment like an adolescent or sophisticated adult. Managing this constant repertoire of haphazard behaviour will test the most patient family. Families acknowledged that the child's normal appearance made it more difficult to be tolerant. They had to remind themselves constantly of the negative factors in the child's background history.

Families with experience of caring for 'hard to place' children felt that the intensity of temper tantrums which they experienced with the abused child was different to anything that they had ever encountered previously. These tantrums were described as 'wild', 'uncontrollable' and 'unpredictable' as children unleashed their anger in a vindictive and destructive manner. Clothing was torn apart, furniture wrecked and windows smashed in the most difficult episodes. The most extreme outbursts are likely to be from children who are unable to verbalize the pain of their abuse. Talking about abuse seemed to channel the pain outwards, leaving children with greater control over their lives. Inability to talk seemed to concentrate the pain internally and it began to burst out in all directions. When preparing families for this arduous task, however, it is important to keep a balanced perspective. With such a daunting catalogue of difficulties it is easy to convey the impression that life with an abused child must be a totally negative experience.

Families were keen to emphasize the rewarding aspects also. Children did make unmistakeable progress, even though this was often gradual and resulted in some families having to revise their original high expectations. Some looked on excitedly as they observed deflated, unconfident, robot-like children blossom as their real personality had the opportunity to express itself. It was unmistakeably clear to most families that there was an immediate connection between all their hard work and significant improvements in the child. Some families thrived on the challenging nature of the task. Perhaps the clearest indication that it was rewarding was the fact that as many as 70 per cent of families felt that they would have no hesitation in taking on another sexually abused child in the future.

OTHER CHILDREN IN THE FAMILY

Other children in the family require preparation too. The concept of sexual abuse is not easy to explain to children and it is therefore tempting to sidestep this issue. Some families may have a natural reticence about discussing straightforward sexual facts with their children. How are they then going to explain sexual aberrations? These are issues which social workers need to address with families. If the family procrastinate on this issue, there is a very strong likelihood that the abused child will undertake this task for them and provide the other children with a rather distorted view of sexual relationships.

Abused children are likely to bring a new awareness of sex into family life. Other children may become intimately involved through sexual touching. Consequently, they need to be alerted to the possibility of this happening and also require guidance about how to react should this occur. Even if sexual touching does not occur, abused children may choose to make their first disclosure to another child. Alternatively, other children may inadvertently be present when a disclosure is made to an adult.

A major preoccupation for families taking on an abused child is likely to be whether their other children will be adversely affected if sexual incidents do occur. Perhaps because this was such a source of concern, the families in this study intervened very quickly and effectively as soon as anything of a sexual nature became apparent. As far as could be ascertained, there did not seem to be any long term difficulties accruing from these sexual episodes.

A much more crucial issue for other children is likely to be the excessive amount of parental time and energy which the abused child will absorb. This inevitably detracts from the amount of attention which can be devoted to them. Prior to placing an abused child in any family, consideration should be given to the emotional stability and maturity of other children. Another important factor is whether adequate physical space exists in the home to allow the other children breathing space from the constant demands of the abused child.

THE IMPACT ON PEOPLE OUTSIDE THE FAMILY

Families not only have to manage their own feelings when abused children exhibit sexual behaviour they also have to handle the responses of relatives, friends, neighbours, tradesmen and any member of the general public. No one is immune from the possibility of being propositioned sexually, inappropriately informed by the child about the intimate details of abuse, subjected to a torrent of sexual words or blatantly interrogated about aspects of their own sex life.

Some families in this study found it essential to take minute care of every aspect of the abused child's life. By thinking ahead, some foster and adoptive parents managed to protect people around them from embarrassing sexual incidents. In these circumstances, families sometimes found themselves subjected to criticism by onlookers who felt that they were over-reacting. It was hard for outsiders to accept that a child who appeared normal required to be treated differently to other children. There were additional pressures associated with having to explain and re-explain methods of parenting which did not conform to normal expectations.

DISCLOSURE

The importance of children being able to talk about their experiences of abuse needs to be stressed. Some families were muddled about how to react when a child began to disclose because they had not received adequate guidance on this matter. Some remained ambivalent about whether they should encourage or discourage open discussion on this sensitive subject. Every family requires simple guidelines on this aspect so that there is no uncertainty about what is expected of them.

Prior to talking, it is usual for children to display signs of abuse through play, sexualized behaviour or inappropriate interaction with other children or adults. It was by being attuned to these indicators and using them as a basis for discussion that many families were gradually able to encourage children to verbalize their stories of abuse.

Listening to children talking about their abuse may stir up a range of emotions such as disbelief, anger and revulsion in foster and adoptive families. Handling these feelings while simultaneously helping the child is inherently stressful. Particularly in extreme cases of abuse, there is always the risk that these feelings may become so overwhelming that they begin to affect other relationships. It is vital that families living through disclosure have someone outside their immediate situation in whom they can confide. This prevents strong feelings from becoming trapped inside the family's four walls and also ensures access to an objective viewpoint on what is happening.

Even when disclosure has occurred prior to placement, some children may not have revealed the full story of their abuse. More details are likely to be shared with the substitute family as the child grows to trust them. This information may involve an enlargement of facts which are already known or new allegations against other perpetrators. It is unhelpful to have rigid ideas about the length of time it may take for a child to talk about abuse. This merely denies the individuality of every child.

Children's ability to share the intimate details of their abuse is likely to have a positive effect on the placement. It was when children felt able to talk about abuse within the foster and adoptive family rather than with a therapist outside the family that the most significant differences occurred. The intensity of behavioural problems subsided. Nightmares, sleeplessness, excessive masturbation and the constant bombardment of sexualized language were just some examples of difficulties which became less pronounced. Children seemed to be capable of more meaningful attachments after verbalizing their story. Disclosure also had the effect of making the foster or adoptive family feel much closer to the child. Being entrusted with such an intimate secret was perceived as an honour. Consequently, placements seemed to have a much higher chance of survival if children managed to tell their new family about their abuse.

Disclosure is not just a single experience with a clear-cut ending. Different stages of development, new events and new crises may open and re-open wounds for abused children years after placement. Substitute families need to be sensitive to this aspect if they are to offer maximum help to abused children.

ALLEGATIONS OF SEXUAL ABUSE AGAINST CARERS

The risk of allegations of sexual abuse is a factor which requires to be discussed with every foster and adoptive family so that they can reflect on any changes in their family lifestyle which may be expedient. Handling day-to-day affairs like personal privacy, nudity, toileting, bathing, sleeping arrangements, childsitting and escorting children which may scarcely have needed a moment's thought in the past may suddenly take on a new meaning when a sexually abused child is integrated into the family. Established ways of working may require to be revised or new family rules introduced to minimize the likelihood of an allegation being made against any family member.

Within the context of this study, it was only possible to interview a small number of families where an allegation of sexual abuse had occurred. This small number demonstrates the vulnerability of foster and adoptive families when they take on a sexually abused child. Each social services department needs to devise a policy statement and clear practice guidelines to deal with this eventuality. Every foster and adoptive family needs to be briefed at an early stage about what to expect from their social services department should an allegation occur. This includes information about departmental procedures which will be instigated and the type of support which they will be offered.

In the event of an allegation occurring, the following points should be carefully considered.

159

a) The relevance of providing the family with an independent worker to support them through this stressful period. The family's own social worker may find it too difficult to continue to support the family while simultaneously managing the conflicts associated with departmental loyalties.
b) The importance of providing help for other children in the family who may be deeply hurt and confused by the experience.
c) The necessity of an ongoing dialogue with the family as the issues surrounding the allegation move from phase to phase.
d) In cases where an allegation is disproved, the family require a written statement from their social services department about the outcome. In addition, they need to know what is recorded on their casefile as this will have relevance for their ongoing work.
e) The protracted length of time that it may take the family to recover from the pain of an allegation and the implications of this for future fostering and adoption work.
f) Every family may find it beneficial to consult the guidelines devised by the National Foster Care Association on the subject of allegations.

THERAPY

The model of therapy used with abused children who have been placed with substitute families needs to be re-examined. In this study the predominant model was one which excluded the substitute family while focusing primarily on an exclusive relationship between the therapist and the abused child. Many families felt angry, frustrated and belittled by this method of working. They resented being excluded from the treatment plan for the child and yet being expected to respond sensitively to children's emotional distress following a therapy session. Several families worried about whether concepts used in therapy sessions like 'secrets', 'locked doors' and 'closed diaries' were merely echoes for children of their original experience of abuse which had often been accompanied with phrases like 'Don't tell anyone' or 'It's a secret'.

The positive value of abused children being able to talk with their foster or adoptive family about their abuse has already been stated. Exclusive therapy which works in isolation from the substitute family tends to block this communication. A reappraisal of this way of working is, therefore, urgently required.

Therapists' reports were not always shared with other professionals working with the child. This had the effect of fragmenting the work and undermining the potential for collaborative working. It also tended to give sexual abuse an exaggerated importance and to isolate it from the child's total range of problems. When social workers do not receive all the relevant information, this reverberates on the foster or adoptive family who are left with unnecessary gaps in their knowledge and understanding of the child.

SUPPORT

Social work support

It is important to build in a framework of social work support from the outset of the placement. When a child is in placement, the most effective method of support is the very traditional approach whereby a social worker visits the family on a regular basis. Some families perceived these visits as their lifeline. Other types of support through one worker bringing several families together on a group basis had certain economic advantages from a professional perspective but was not an adequate substitute for home visits.

Social workers have a variety of functions to perform:

a) listening to and absorbing some of the family's pain;
b) offering direction to the family about handling difficult behaviour, and about how to undertake sex education with an abused child;
c) recognizing the family's need for access to other professionals or specialist services and ensuring that appropriate links are established.

In fostering placements, the availability of two social workers is essential – one to focus on the abused child's needs, the other to support the family. As this study illustrates, abused children are capable of the most disruptive influence on family life. Families need time for themselves if the ongoing quality of their family life is to be retained.

The gender of the social worker is important. Some foster carers or adopters may struggle with their own sexuality or experience sexual problems with a partner. Some people in this study had difficulty discussing such intimate aspects of their lives with a social worker of the opposite sex. Consideration should therefore always be given to the influence of the gender of the social worker on the placement.

A 24-hour support service is essential. The normal out of hours service is unlikely to meet the needs of struggling families. It was criticized because of delays in responses and the unhelpfulness of having an unfamiliar worker who often lacked specialist knowledge or understanding about sexually abused children in family placement. Families who were given their social worker's home telephone number for use in an emergency expressed a much higher degree of satisfaction. Having access to this telephone number was a psychological boost which often enabled families to hold on throughout an emergency and defer telephoning until the following working day.

Important professional services

Three particular professional services stand out as being especially significant for families:

a) Access to a specialist

Most families preferred to obtain direct access to a person who could offer specialist advice on sexual abuse rather than reading current literature. Who can they consult? Social Workers, psychologists, psychiatrists and psychotherapists are potential sources of specialist knowledge. Within the context of this study, few social workers were specialists in this field. One problem is that there is no easily identifiable location where families can turn for information about child sexual abuse as it affects substitute families. Consequently, they are dependent on their social worker making a referral to a specialist on their behalf. In order to do this effectively, social workers need to be knowledgeable about resources. This study demonstrates that families were largely in a 'hit and miss' situation. Some got access to helpful advice by chance rather than by design. Even when they did find a professional with expertise in sexual abuse, there was no guarantee that such a person would ever have had the opportunity to grapple with the essential differences between counselling a birth family and a substitute family.

As the numbers of children coming into care are increasingly being identified as victims of sexual abuse, there is a need for easily identifiable information in relation to re-parenting such children. More and more professionals are jumping on the sexual abuse bandwagon and declaring themselves to be 'experts'. Who assesses the credibility of such specialists? Would it be unrealistic to hope that some agency with specialist experience in substitute family care and child sexual abuse might establish a project as a resource to which professionals and substitute families could turn for consultation and direction in relation to adoption and fostering of abused children?

b) Help from a psychologist

The advantage of working on a specific programme for modifying behaviour is that it enables the entire family to work collaboratively in an organized and consistent manner rather than on a trial and error basis. This inspires hope and reduces the likelihood of families feeling swamped as weeks change to months of facing the same, seemingly intractable problems.

Getting access to a psychologist proved to be difficult for many of the families who took part in this study. Frequently, the family reached crisis point or the placement was moving rapidly towards disruption before this was forthcoming.

This study points to the need for every statutory and voluntary agency to take cognisance of the fact that access to a psychologist is one resource which families re-parenting sexually abused children are likely to require. It is unhelpful if social workers initiate their search for this facility at a point of crisis. It is preferable to ensure that this service forms part of a total package of services available to every foster and adoptive family who want to benefit from it.

c) Respite care

The availability of respite care is crucial for every family undertaking this challenging task. There is a need to increase respite provision to meet current demand. The fact that some foster and adoptive families may choose not to use this resource should not preclude them from this offer. One factor which this study highlights is that it is unrealistic to expect foster and adoptive families to receive adequate practical relief through their own social circle of relatives, friends and neighbours. A few families did enthuse about the practical help which they were able to obtain through their own informal networks, but they were the exception rather than the rule. Relatives and friends who were able to help most were usually people who already had specialist experience of working with difficult children.

Foster and adoptive families who used respite care were enthusiastic about its value. Some were fortunate enough to have an established respite care scheme operating in their local area. Others, using their own initiative recruited their own respite carer and then managed to persuade their social services department to pay for it. In one area, a number of foster carers who were members of a local support group introduced their own reciprocal respite care scheme. Some families who yearned for respite care felt cheated because their social services department was unable to provide this facility, even although some had been offered it in theory at the point of planning the placement.

Respite care should not be a crisis-orientated service as was frequently the case in this study. Sometimes the family struggled over a protracted period or the placement came close to collapse before the family's pleas for respite were taken seriously. Respite care takes on a new meaning when it is automatically available as a right to every family from the outset of the placement. Some families feared that the abused child might perceive respite care as a further rejection. They might have viewed this differently if it had been feasible to work constructively with the abused child towards incorporating respite care into their lifestyle from the first day of the placement.

The principle of self-help

The idea of substitute families deriving support through contact with each other is not new. Most families who had immediate access to others in a similar situation to themselves enthused about the benefits. It was, therefore, surprising to discover that some statutory and voluntary agencies ignored the positive aspects of self-help and encouraged families to look for support solely through professional sources. Closing the door on self-help, therefore, constitutes a loss for families.

Foster carers had no major difficulties in making contact with other experienced carers. The availability of local support groups facilitated this. Adopters were much less fortunate. They found it difficult to identify other adopters with experience of parenting abused children. Confidentiality played a part in this. Naturally, adopters were reticent to reveal their child's history of sexual abuse. Consequently, it was difficult for them to know how to locate others with experience of sexual abuse unless their social worker was willing to play a part in ensuring that these introductions occurred. Time and energy invested by professionals in this way would undoubtedly have been time well spent, culminating in additional support for families.

PARTNERSHIP: THE WAY FORWARD

In any work with sexually abused children, the concept of partnership between substitute families and professionals is of paramount importance. In theory, it is easy for everyone to acknowledge the importance of this principle. In practice, positive examples are harder to find. As this study draws to a conclusion, because professional rivalries and power struggles have tended to predominate, it is imperative to emphasize again how vitally important it is that everyone surrounding the abused child strives to work together. Nobody holds a monopoly of knowledge on this sensitive subject. Statutory and voluntary agencies need to work effectively together. Professionals in various disciplines, acknowledging their differing perspectives, need to learn to trust each others' skills. Information requires to be shared in a co-operative manner with due regard to confidentiality. Foster and adoptive parents are key people in this partnership with specialist skills and unique opportunities to influence children whose lives have been traumatized by sexual abuse. In a study which has concentrated so much on the experiences of people involved in the day to day care of abused children, it seems appropriate to allow an experienced foster carer to offer a final word of advice:

We all have to learn to go ahead as a team – feeling our way stage by stage – learning from experience – foraging all the time for anything new that we can learn about sexually abused children. Sometimes we will have to accept that there are no easy answers. None of us can justify not using the experience that we have acquired. I say to professionals 'You must be there by our side as we move forward – listening, talking, learning – that is the only way to keep walking forward together'.

Recommended books/resources

This is not intended to be a comprehensive book list. It includes only the books and resources which foster and adoptive families who took part in this study found useful.

BOOKS/VIDEOS FOR CHILDREN OR TEENAGERS THAT EXPLORE KEEPING SAFE

ADAMS, FAITH and MARTIN, *No Is Not Enough – Helping Teenagers Avoid Sexual Assault*, Impact Publishers, California, 1984.
ELLIOT, MICHELLE, *Kidscape Training Kit*, Kidscape, London.
(Some siblings were going through a Kidscape Programme at school at the time when a sexually abused child joined their family.)
ELLIOT, MICHELLE, *Preventing Child Sexual Assault*, Bedford Square Press, London, 1985.
FREEMAN, LORY, *Loving Touches*, Parenting Press Incorporated, Seattle USA, 1986.
HESSELL and NELSON, *I'm Glad I Told Mum*, Beaver Books, London, 1988.
Feeling Safe – Feeling Strong, Lerner Publications Co, Minneapolis USA, 1984.
HINDMAN, JAN, *A Very Touching Book*, McLure Hindman Associates, Oregon, 1984.
(Several families found this book excellent for helping children talk about their experiences of sexual abuse.)
PITHERS and GREEN, *We Can say No*, Arrow Books, London, 1984.
VIZARD, EILEEN, *Self-Esteem and Personal Safety*, Great Ormond Street Hospital, London, 1986.

(Videotape, notes and twelve picture flashcards used in group work for very young victims of sexual abuse.)
HARRIS, ROLF, Kids Can Say No (video).
(After watching this video at a Training Course for foster carers, two carers disclosed details of their own abuse for the first time.)

ACTIVITY BOOKS

It's OK to Say No – colouring book and activity book,
Published by Peter Haddock Ltd, Bridlington, 1985.
STRIKER, SUSAN, *The Anti Colouring Book*, Hippo Books, Scholastic Publications, London, 1989.

GROWING UP

MAYLE, PETER, *Where Did I Come From?* MacMillan, London (book now out of print). Animated video available.
MAYLE, PETER, *What's Happening To Me?* MacMillan, London (currently being reprinted). Animated video available.
RAYNER, CLAIRE, *The Body Book*, Pan Books, Basingstoke, 1979.

CHILDREN'S STORY BOOKS (DEALING WITH SEXUAL ABUSE)

ROUF, KHADJ, *Mousie* (suitable for children aged 4–9 years).
ROUF, KHADJ, *Secrets* (suitable for children aged 8–16 years).
ROUF, KHADJ and PEAKE, ANNE, *My Book – My Body* (suitable for children aged 4–12 years).
Holding His Mask – written by teenage victims of abuse (for teenagers).
Note: The above four books form part of *Working with Sexually Abused Children – A Resource Pack for Professionals*, Children's Society, London, 1988.
WACHTER, ORALEE, *No More Secrets for Me*, Viking Kestrel, Britain, 1985 (age 6–15 years).
ELLIOT, MICHELLE, *Willow Street Kids*, Andre Deutsch/Pan Piccolo, London, 1986 (age 7–11 years).

AUTOBIOGRAPHIES (FOR ADULTS – ABOUT VICTIMS OF SEXUAL ABUSE)

FRASER, SYLVIA, *My Father's House*, Virago Press Ltd, London 1989.
SPRING, JACQUELINE, *Cry Hard and Swim*, Virago Press Ltd, London, 1988.

CHILDREN'S BOOKS – BEREAVEMENT

KREMENTZ, GILL, *How It feels When A Parent Dies*, Victor Gollancz, London, 1988. (Much wider relevance than death. Can be used with children coming into care.)
VARLEY, SUSAN, *Badger's Parting Gift*, Picture Lions, Britain, 1984.
WILHELM, HANS, *I'll Always Love You*, Crown Publishers, New York, 1985.

CHILDREN'S BOOKS (PARTICULARLY RELEVANT FOR CHILDREN IN CARE)

AHLBERG, ALLAN and MCNAUGHTON, COLIN, *Families*, Studio Publications, Ipswich, 1986.
DAVIS, DIANE, *Something is Wrong at My House*, Parenting Press, Seattle, 1984.
HARRIOTT, TED, *Coming Home – A Dog's True Story* Lynx, London, 1988.
HOLLICK, HELEN, *Come and Tell Me*, Dinosaur, London, 1986.
LIVINGSTONE, CAROL, *Why Was I Adopted?* Angus and Robertson, London, 1980.
ORAM and KITAMURA, *Angry Arthur*, Penguin, London, 1984.
PRESTON, *The Temper Tantrum Book*, Penguin Picture Puffin, London, 1987.
THOM and MCLIVER, *Bruce's Story*, Children's Society, London, 1986.

GENERAL BOOKS (FOR ADULTS)

FAHLBERG, VERA, *Fitting the Pieces Together*, BAAF, London, 1988.

In Touch With Children Training Pack, BAAF, London, 1984.

JEWETT, CLAUDIA, *Helping Children Cope with Separation and Loss*, Batsford, London, 1982.

OAKLANDER, VIOLET, *Windows to our Children* Real People Press, Utah 84532 USA, 1978.

ROWLANDS, PETER, *Saturday Parent*, Allen and Unwin, London, 1980.

Index